FBI Surveillance Tape
April 29, 1993
3:53 P.M.

STANFA: The only one I tell is you. And you gonna keep it quiet and we see. In the meantime, we look and see. We got a good shot, fine. We no got a good shot, we wait . . . We gotta be real careful.

SERGIO BATTAGLIA: Beautiful. Kill 'em. F— 'em. Kill right there. Put 'em in the Dumpster. Cement it. Put 'em in the trunk . . . One of 'em, maybe we'll take to New York. One down to Delaware. We spread 'em out.

STANFA: We put in a little concrete . . . See, they got already mixed concrete. In the bag, already mixed . . . Soon as we do it, we put it over there. We put it in the trunk all night. Wait all night somewhere . . . This way the concrete hardens and we'll go dump 'em.

BATTAGLIA: Yea, that's no problem. The mountains is good . . . We got to get two of 'em. That's probably the good way. All three, we work it right . . . Oh, this is gonna work beautiful.

THE
GOODFELLA
TAPES

GEORGE ANASTASIA

AVON BOOKS
An Imprint of HarperCollins*Publishers*

THE GOODFELLA TAPES is a journalistic account of the actual investigation and conviction of several organized crime figures in and around Philadelphia, Pennsylvania, from 1990 to 1995. The events recounted in the book are true. Scenes and dialogue have been reconstructed based on formal interviews, local and federal law enforcement records, and published news stories. Quoted testimony and other court-related statements from before, during, and after trial have been taken verbatim from transcripts.

AVON BOOKS
An Imprint of HarperCollins*Publishers*
10 East 53rd Street
New York, New York 10022-5299

Copyright © 1998 by George Anastasia
Library of Congress Catalog Card Number: 97-94928
ISBN: 0-380-79637-6
www.avonbooks.com

First Avon Books printing: May 1998

Avon Trademark Reg. U.S. Pat. Off. and in Other Countries, Marca Registrada, Hecho en U.S.A.
HarperCollins® is a trademark of HarperCollins Publishers Inc.

Printed in the U.S.A.

10 9 8 7 6

*For my mother
and in memory
of my father,
with love*

Author's Note and Acknowledgments

Back in October of 1996, jailed Philadelphia mobster Sergio Battaglia called me on the phone to apologize. The young would-be hit man said he wanted me to know that he was sorry, that it was nothing personal when he was plotting with mob boss John Stanfa to kill me a few years ago.

Battaglia, who is now cooperating with the government, also said he was glad that the plot never got beyond the talking stage.

"Thankfully, nothing happened," he said in a brief telephone conversation from a federal prison.

I didn't know what to say.

"Sure, no hard feelings," didn't seem to cover it.

"Yeah, I understand," didn't make sense.

Because even if I accept the fact that John Stanfa headed one of the most incompetent groups of misfit would-be murderers ever inducted into La Cosa Nostra, there *are* hard feelings.

And I don't understand.

Maybe I've been at this too long.

Maybe a dozen years of writing about wiseguys warps the brain.

I used to think there was a code of conduct in the underworld, that the reason it was called "organized" crime was because it was *organized*; that there was a structure with clearly defined rules within which mobsters operated. And so whenever anyone would ask if I worried about my own safety, I would offer a stock answer, mumbling something about the unwritten understanding that wiseguys never targeted cops, prosecutors, or reporters—as long as they were doing their jobs honestly.

Then I'd tell a story about Spike, a wannabe wiseguy from the 1980s who was an underworld sycophant of former Philadelphia mob boss Nicodemo "Little Nicky" Scarfo. Spike contacted me just before a book I had written on Scarfo mob soldier Nick Caramandi was published. Spike, who cooked, cleaned and maintained Scarfo's lavish hacienda in Fort Lauderdale during the diminutive mob boss's brief reign as Mafia kingpin, wanted to know if I'd be interested in writing a book about him. Unfortunately, most of the stories he told were covered by Caramandi, so I passed.

A few weeks later, after the Caramandi book came out, Spike called me at the office. He ranted and raved, threatened to kill me, told me he was going to get a hatchet and split my head open, get a gun and shoot me between the eyes. He then went on to berate my writing style and question my manhood.

The harangue lasted twenty minutes. I said very little. Then Spike hung up.

I took solace in the fact that Spike had had to reverse the charges—had to call me collect—in order to make these threats. A week later he called back to apologize, claiming he was drunk and broke and really didn't mean anything by it.

"Sure, no hard feelings. I understand," I said.

That was five years ago.

Battaglia's call was another matter.

He was in the protective custody wing of a federal prison awaiting sentencing. He had been convicted with Stanfa and six other mobsters back in November of 1995 on racketeering and conspiracy charges that included murder, murder conspiracy, kidnapping, arson, extortion, and obstruction of justice.

The plot to murder me was not part of the case.

I covered the trial, which lasted nearly three months. I would nod hello to the defendants each morning when they were brought into the courtroom in handcuffs. Occasionally, I even exchanged pleasantries with Stanfa, who paid me what I considered a high compliment early on when he told me, "Once in a while, you get it right."

At another point he thanked me for a somewhat sympathetic story about a friend of his who had been ordered out of the courtroom during the trial for allegedly giving the *malòcchio* to a government witness. And he seemed genuinely pleased and grateful when I didn't hype a story about the romance between his beautiful young daughter, Sara, and hit man-turned-government-witness Rosario Bellocchi that surfaced while Bellocchi was testifying.

THAT'S AMORE, read the headline in my competitor, *The Philadelphia Daily News*, the next day. The story, with an accompanying FBI surveillance photo of the two young lovers kissing, was apparently a bit too personal for the mob boss's taste.

And in a certain sense—since I am the father of two daughters—I understood. Stanfa was a cold and ruthless mob boss, so he was fair game for both the prosecutors and the media. Those were the rules we all played by. But his daughter was an innocent, and so a certain respect had to be paid. You didn't ignore the story, but you tried to show some compassion. That's the way I felt, anyway, and I think it was reflected in the way I wrote my piece that day.

So I thought I had this relationship with Stanfa. I thought that, on some level, we respected one another.

During the trial I got to know—and even like—some of the family members of the defendants. I felt for them when the guilty verdicts were returned. Most knew that their loved ones would be in jail for the rest of their lives and that they, as wives, parents, brothers or sisters, were sentenced to years of mind-numbing prison visits filled with tears of self-pity and anger.

Like I said, the plot to kill me wasn't part of the racketeering case.

In fact, the feds say they didn't know about it until Battaglia decided to cooperate, which came several weeks after he, Stanfa, and the six others were found guilty. Facing a possible sixty-year jail sentence, Battaglia, who was just twenty-nine years old, cut a deal.

And started singing.

Much of what he had to say reinforced and corroborated the testimony of several other mob turncoats. But the new information included allegations that back in 1993 Stanfa wanted him to kill two prominent Philadelphia defense lawyers—Don Marino and Joe Santaguida—and me.

Battaglia said Stanfa was upset with the way Marino

and Santaguida handled some legal matters for his associates. Marino had had the temerity to ask about being paid for the work he did. Santaguida had the misfortune to represent a Stanfa rival.

As for me, Battaglia said Stanfa was upset with some of the articles I was writing at the time, articles that he thought held him and his organization up to ridicule during a bloody 1993 mob war in which the Stanfa organization gave new meaning to the phrase "the gang that couldn't shoot straight."

Battaglia said Stanfa told him to get some grenades, find out where I lived, and throw them through my window.

As it turned out, Battaglia said, by the time he got the grenades, Stanfa was in the midst of an all-out mob war with a group of young South Philadelphia corner boys. By that point, I was not a priority.

Not a priority.

Nothing personal.

I've got a wife and two daughters. Any one of them, or all three, could have been in the room when the grenade came through the window.

"I just wanted you to know I'm sorry," Battaglia said when he called from jail. "I'm glad it never happened."

So am I.

But don't ask me to understand.

And don't tell me it was nothing personal.

This book grew in large part out of reporting I did for the *Philadelphia Inquirer* during the rise and fall of John Stanfa. And in that regard I would like to acknowledge and thank the work of several current and former editors at the paper who will recognize much of what follows. These would include Dan Biddle, Matt Golas, Rick Lyman, and Dave Tucker.

I would also like to thank those in law enforcement who took the time to share their thoughts and insights with me. While it would be impossible to acknowledge them all, I would be remiss not to mention federal prosecutors Joel Friedman, Barry Gross, Bob Courtney, and Paul Mansfield; FBI agents Jim Maher and Paul Hayes Jr.; former agent Gary Langan; retired Philadelphia Police Captain John Apeldorn; Inspector Vince DeBlasis of the Philadelphia Police Department; Bob Buccino of the New Jersey Attorney General's Division of Criminal Justice; and Philadelphia Deputy Police Commissioner Rich Zappile.

Special thanks to Robert Drake, my agent, who worked tirelessly to find this book a home. And finally, and as always, thanks to my wife, Angela, and daughters, Michelle and Nina, for their love, encouragement and support.

—George Anastasia
January 1997

THE
GOODFELLA
TAPES

Prologue

FBI Surveillance Tape
April 29, 1993
3:53 P.M.

JOHN STANFA: The only one I tell is you. And you gonna
keep it quiet and we see. In the meantime, we look and
see. We got a good shot, fine. We no got a good shot,
we wait. . . . We gotta be real careful.

SERGIO BATTAGLIA: Beautiful. Kill 'em. Fuck 'em. Kill
right there. Put 'em in the Dumpster. Cement it. Put
'em in the trunk. . . . One of 'em, maybe we'll take to
New York. One down to Delaware. We spread 'em out.

STANFA: We put a little concrete. . . . See, they got already mixed concrete. In the bag, already mixed. . . .
Soon as we do it, we put it over there. We put it in the
trunk all night. Wait all night somewhere. . . . This
way the concrete hardens and we'll go dump them.

BATTAGLIA: Yeah, that's no problem. The mountains is
good. . . . We got to get two of them. That's probably
the good way. All three, we work it right. . . . Oh, this
is gonna work beautiful.

The jurors sat dumbfounded as the words of the two
mobsters echoed around the high-ceilinged courtroom.

1

Occasionally one would steal a glance at Stanfa, the bull-necked mob boss from Sicily who had taken over the Philadelphia crime family, or Battaglia, the baby-faced young mob soldier. Seated with their lawyers and co-defendants at the L-shaped defense table, neither showed any emotion as their words—a conspiracy to murder three mob rivals—hung in the air.

STANFA: Fuck, I got to put one right here with my very own hands . . . in the mouth, motherfucker. . . . You know what I'll do. I'll get a knife. . . . I'll cut out his tongue and we'll send it to the wife. That's all. . . . We put it in an envelope. Put a stamp on it.
BATTAGLIA: That's it.
STANFA: Honest to God.
BATTAGLIA: That's it. I think it's good.

This was in October 1995, in a seventeenth-floor courtroom of the United States District Courthouse in Philadelphia. Nine weeks and 178 tapes later, the jury found Stanfa, Battaglia, and six co-defendants guilty of all counts, an assorted racketeering grab-bag that included four murders, fourteen murder conspiracies, one arson, a kidnapping, and a dozen extortions.

STANFA: I'm a greaseball? I show who's. . . . They think because we come from over there, we're bigger fools than them. . . . Fifteen minutes, twenty minutes . . . that's all we need. What's going on? What's the problem? Tatatatata. . . . You gotta hit them when they don't expect no problem. . . . See, you no gotta give a chance. Pam, pam. You no gotta give no fucking chance. . . . Over here. Over here it's the best. Behind the ear.
BATTAGLIA: Maybe next week we get everything ready.

The mop, the radio, the gloves. Everything. Everything's there.

STANFA: They're supposed to have some acid, you know. Fuck. It eats everything.

BATTAGLIA: I just want to pour it on his hands . . . his face, his eyes, everything.

STANFA: Motherfucker.

This is the story of the rise of mob boss John Stanfa and the unprecedented federal investigation that brought him down. The story is played out against the backdrop of a bloody mob war that rocked South Philadelphia in 1993.

The violence, the plotting, the treachery are typical of most mob stories. What is different is the FBI presence from start to finish. This was a mob war that the feds had wired. They got most of it on tape. Some of it on video.

The feds had a bug in the law office of Stanfa's criminal defense attorney, Salvatore J. Avena, for nearly two years. More than two thousand conversations were recorded. Mob leaders from three different families, including Sal Profaci—son of the late New York Colombo family boss Joe Profaci—were picked up offering candid comments and detailed accounts of Mafia life.

"Goodfellas don't sue goodfellas . . . goodfellas kill goodfellas," said Profaci, in one unguarded comment that quickly became the signature phrase of the investigation.

"I was born and raised in This Thing," Stanfa said in another conversation in which he complained about the younger generation of American mobster, "and I'm gonna die in This Thing. But with the right people. . . . Over here, it's like kindergarten."

Stanfa, the tough-talking mobster who rose to the top of one of the most violent Mafia families in America, emerged from the tapes as a cross between King Lear and Don Corleone, alternately brutally violent and irrationally paranoid as his battle with a group of young wiseguys headed by the charismatic Joseph "Skinny Joey" Merlino raged across the streets of South Philadelphia.

The cultural and generational clash between the fifty-year-old Sicilian-born Stanfa and the thirty-year-old South Philadelphia street corner–bred Merlino sparked a series of conversations in which veteran mobsters talked wistfully about the old days and lamented the demise of the American Mafia.

This is also a story about the modern mob and about the cast of characters—refugees from a Quentin Tarantino movie, it seemed—who found their way to the Stanfa organization. There was the hit man who once used an electric power drill to torture a rival and who, after joining the organization, renamed his pit bull "Al Capone." And the former nude go-go dancer recruited to slip poison into Merlino's cocktail. And the assassin who blew a murder opportunity because he had placed the wrong size shells in his sawed-off shotgun.

There was also a murderous love triangle that bloomed in the midst of the bloody mob war when two young Stanfa hit men both fell in love with his daughter. Their courtship of the dark-haired and achingly beautiful Mafia princess led to a bungled hit, a botched kidnapping, and a car chase right out of the movies.

The FBI investigation into the Stanfa organization also opened a window into the inner workings of La Cosa Nostra nationwide. Information gathered during the probe, which lasted nearly four years, is still being used by agents and US Attorneys in Philadelphia, Manhattan, Brooklyn, and Newark to build additional cases.

There were a series of meetings in which Profaci outlined the mob's role in controlling the multimillion-dollar trash disposal business. There were several conversations in which he and Stanfa discussed how to fix prices and control the distribution of pasta products on supermarket shelves and cheese sold to pizzerias from Philadelphia to New York. There was detailed information about the bloody mob war that rocked New York's Colombo Family and left more than a dozen wiseguys dead and an equal number wounded. And there was Profaci's plaintive declaration that his late father, the former boss of the family, would be "rolling in his grave" if he could see what was happening to his beloved Cosa Nostra.

Finally, there was the wanton and rampant violence of Philadelphia in 1993, including the predawn hit on Stanfa's underboss, Joe Ciancaglini Jr. The shooting, in a small luncheonette, was recorded on audio and video by the FBI, who had the joint under surveillance. This is *the only time a mob hit has ever been recorded in progress*.

After every major event, the FBI heard Stanfa, Profaci, or some other key player discuss the incident, offering advice or counsel, swearing revenge or lamenting the loss of honor, value, and loyalty that once were the cornerstones of their organization. Their words offer a spellbinding take on "the life" and a fascinating insight into those who live it.

*   *   *

This is also a story of disorganized organized crime; a sad, frightening, funny and violent tale about an often glamorized institution reduced to graphically bloody comic book terms.

At one point, the feds heard Sal Avena complain to an associate about federal investigators. Avena said he had his office swept for bugs on a regular basis.

It was expensive, Avena said.

"But it's money well spent," said Avena's associate as the undetected listening device beamed the conversation back to the FBI's listening post a block away.

The jury had all that and more when it began deliberating. On November 21, 1995, six days after it got the case, it came back with a verdict. Stanfa, Battaglia, crime family underboss Frank Martines, consigliere Anthony "Tony Buck" Piccolo, mob capos Salvatore "Shotsie" Sparacio and Vincent "Al Pajamas" Pagano, mob soldier Raymond Esposito and mob associate Herb Keller were convicted of racketeering and racketeering conspiracy. The defendants, all being held without bail, faced sentences of from thirty years to life.

FBI Surveillance Tape
April 30, 1993
9:49 A.M.

STANFA: Tony, believe me . . . this thing, this is my headache right now.
ANTHONY PICCOLO: Sure.
STANFA: See. . . . from Mister Nice Guy, I'm gonna be Mister Bad Guy.
PICCOLO: You have to.
STANFA: Everybody, they gotta walk in line. The first one that make a mistake, fuck them. . . . See, you be a nice

guy, they do this and take your arms, too. Forget about it.

SALVATORE SPARACIO: They, they got everything by the balls anyhow. They got nothing to gain by creating a problem. . . . Look how much they doing.

PICCOLO: Sam, they're no good . . . they're no good.

STANFA: Me, you, him. Old timers. That's a different way. They got a different school. Everything. These people, they think of one thing. . . . No respect. Nothing. They no have a respect on you, your family.

SPARACIO: Nobody. . . . No respect.

PICCOLO: They don't have it. . . . They don't have it.

SPARACIO: Loyalty. There's not loyalty from the beginning. I never felt so uncomfortable in my . . . fifty years. Before, you swore with your back up. I watch your back, you watch my back. There was never no problem.

STANFA: I got a family, too. I worry about my son. I worry about everybody. . . . Listen, they don't hear no speech. Believe me, they don't hear no speech. . . . That's it. So, anyway, this is the situation. . . . In other words, all three, they gotta go. Then, what we, you do, forget about it, you know?

PICCOLO: It's the only way. All right, Sam?

SPARACIO: Sure, if it's, uh, you know. . . . We have to.

PICCOLO: They could take us all out. . . . They want to take us all out.

STANFA: I know. Because, see, that's what they want to do. They want control.

1

It started in the fall of 1990 on the campus of La Salle University. With the college clock chiming in the background, Eddie O'Hanlon, an accounting student $3,925 in debt to a mob bookmaker, met with Tommy Morrone, a bulky young collector for the organization.

Morrone, the twenty-two-year-old son of an imprisoned gangster, was alternately perplexed, annoyed, and dumbfounded over O'Hanlon's inability to come up with the money he had lost betting baseball playoff games that weekend.

O'Hanlon, a thin, twenty-year-old undergraduate from the suburbs, was in turn broke, scared, and begging for more time.

He was also wired for sound.

As a result, the first words the FBI heard in a four-year investigation that would bring down Philadelphia mob boss John Stanfa and most of his organization were recorded at 9:11 A.M. on October 25, 1990.

Morrone, a six-foot-two, 280-pound wannabe wiseguy, dominated the conversation.

"You went in and you bet thirty-nine hundred this week with no fuckin' money?" he asked O'Hanlon as they sat outside a lecture hall on the tree-lined campus located in the city's Olney section. "I mean, are you out of your fuckin' mind or what? You're not playin' with little kids here."

"I'm scared to death right now," O'Hanlon said. "I mean, I didn't even think . . ."

"It's not a matter of bein' scared," Morrone shot back, not giving O'Hanlon time to finish his thought. "It's a matter you gotta get the fuckin' money. . . . They want the fuckin' money. They don't wanna know nothin'. That's what they said to me. That they don't wanna know nothin'. I mean, how, how do you bet . . . with no fuckin' money at all? I don't understand it. You gotta be outta your mind."

Over the next four years, federal and state organized crime investigators would secretly record 2,000 more conversations as the gambling probe that started that morning expanded. First, a bookmaking ring headed by Morrone's boss, "Shotsie" Sparacio, was targeted. Phones were tapped and a bug was placed in a South Jersey bakery where Sparacio did his business.

Within a year, however, the FBI and the US Attorney's office in Philadelphia realized they were on to something more. Morrone's big mouth and Sparacio's wheeling and dealing led to a law office in Camden, New Jersey, where mob leaders from three different crime families had begun meeting on a regular basis. With court approval, the office was bugged and what had started as a gambling probe became a major racketeering investigation.

From a cramped listening post in the basement of the federal courthouse a block away, FBI agents monitoring the meetings got it all—in candid, profane, and often humorous detail—from the mouths of some of the men they considered to be top Mafia figures in the America.

There was Salvatore J. Profaci, a capo in New York's Colombo crime family and the son of late mob boss Joe Profaci. And William ''Big Billy'' D'Elia, allegedly a major figure in the Scranton-Wilkes Barre branch of La Cosa Nostra once headed by his mentor, Russell Bufalino. There was Tomaso Gambino, the young son of a convicted Sicilian Mafia heroin dealer. And, of course, there were Stanfa, Sparacio, Piccolo, and a handful of other local mob figures.

''Most of our major mob cases start out as gambling investigations,'' said FBI agent James T. Maher, a veteran of the Philadelphia mob wars who supervised the bugging operation and who, by the time Stanfa went to trial, was supervisor of the organized crime squad. ''This one was no different.''

''At the time, we didn't know where this was going to take us,'' added Barry Gross, the Assistant US Attorney who coordinated most of the taping activity. ''It was Eddie O'Hanlon's father who made him come to us. And it just kept going from there.''

In the aftermath, when all the tapes had been played and the witnesses had testified and the jury had delivered its verdict, there were those who said the feds had been incredibly lucky—that they had stumbled onto an investigation and had hit a jackpot by chance. And, to be sure, there was some of that in the case. But it was another Philadelphian a long time ago, a guy named Ben Franklin, who coined a phrase that best sums up the long, hard, and at times mind-numbingly tedious law enforcement work that went into making the Stanfa case.

"It's amazing," Franklin supposedly said. "The harder I work, the luckier I get."

"This is, this is unbelievable," Morrone said. "Unreal. . . . You gotta, you gotta just make sure you're around every day and you gotta, you gotta come up with somethin', you have to. . . . You know what I mean? They're not gonna give you too much time. Go see. See what you could do. Go see everybody you know. Grab somethin' from somebody."

"I told my parents and they just said, 'No,'" O'Hanlon said. "You know, 'This is your problem.' And right now, I'm just probably about to get kicked out of the house. . . . I don't think it's hit 'em yet what's really goin' on, but, you know, with me owin' these people this money. I don't think that they really realize what. . . . 'cause I was tellin' 'em. . . . cause I was holdin' them out to the last resort."

"Well, you better tell them it's fuckin' serious," Morrone shot back. "I gotta go face these people tonight and tell 'em this fuckin' kid don't have the money. They're gonna go absolutely crazy."

O'Hanlon had been betting for several weeks. He was making his plays through a fellow student, Nick Perna. Perna was a friend of Morrone's, and had gotten the number of a South Philadelphia bookmaking operation from him.

Like anything else, it was networking—who you knew and who they knew. And it was incredibly easy. Make the call. Give the right name so that the guy on the other end of the line knows you're legitimate and that someone is vouching for you. Place the bet. Collect your winnings. The week before, O'Hanlon had won

$1,600, a fact that was not lost on Morrone during the discussion that fall morning.

"You won sixteen hundred. Whatcha do with that?" Morrone asked.

"That was for my friend," O'Hanlon said. He had called for a fellow classmate, who had taken the money and given it to his parents for next semester's tuition, O'Hanlon explained.

None of that mattered to Morrone or to the people he represented.

"You was happy callin' in them fuckin' bets," Morrone told a nervous O'Hanlon. "I mean, it's unbelievable. You was nice and happy when you were callin' the fuck in. Now, all of a sudden, what, what am I gonna do? . . . You know what I mean. You wanna bet. You wanna act like a fuckin' man, you gotta be like a man now. You gotta come up with the fuckin' money somehow."

O'Hanlon asked for time. He said he'd try to raise the money. He said he had a project to turn in, a lecture to get to. He wanted to end the discussion, get away from the hulking mobster. In the background, students could be heard walking to their next class. The college chimes were ringing again. It was a strange setting, given the topic of conversation: the underworld and the undergraduate, a clash of cultures; people who didn't belong together, thrown together; people talking different languages, hearing but not listening to each other. While no one realized it at the time, this collision of divergent interests would be a theme that repeated itself throughout the Stanfa investigation.

But for now it was just the start of a gambling probe.

"They're gonna be like fuckin' maniacs tonight,"

Morrone said. "Especially that they paid, that they gave you sixteen hundred last week. Wait til I tell 'em this tonight . . . that you don't have nothin'. . . . They're gonna go absolutely crazy."

"You're meetin' these guys tonight?" O'Hanlon asked.

"Yeah . . . the worst part . . . you're empty-handed," Morrone said. "You don't have nothin' to offer them. You know what I mean? You can't even make them a deal and say, well, I'll give you fuckin' five hundred. . . ."

"I gotta talk to these guys and tell 'em," O'Hanlon said.

"Whatta ya think the guys are gonna say to you?" asked Morrone. "They're gonna say 'Fuck you,' that's what they're gonna say."

For ten more minutes, Morrone and O'Hanlon went around the same circle. O'Hanlon wanted time and said he'd try to raise the money. Morrone said he should have thought about that before, and then berated the ertswhile gambler for betting on baseball to begin with.

"Baseball's all fuckin' streaks, man. . . . That's all baseball is, it's fuckin' streaks."

Gambling, on the other hand, was business. That was the bottom line for Morrone. So he left O'Hanlon with this:

"All's I can say is, if you don't come up with somethin' soon, you're gonna be in a fuckin' lotta trouble. Big, big trouble. You're gonna be . . . you're gonna get hurt. That's all. I mean, you really are. That's what's gonna happen. You're gonna get hurt. You're gonna get hurt bad. . . ."

*　　*　　*

By the time Morrone met with O'Hanlon, the FBI had already paid a visit to Nick Perna, O'Hanlon's classmate and campus gambling contact. The feds convinced the stocky, young bookie that he, too, should cooperate. Over the next several months Perna wore a body wire to a series of meetings with Morrone and Sparacio in which he used cash supplied by the FBI to pay down O'Hanlon's gambling debt.

The feds also tapped the phones of the bookmakers in South Philadelphia who took O'Hanlon's action, and on Christmas Day, two months after that first conversation on the La Salle campus, they planted a bug in the office of the Deluxe Italian Bakery in Runnemede, New Jersey, where Morrone had taken Perna to meet Sparacio.

Christmas was one of the few days that the bakery was closed.

There was at least some thought that Sparacio, a long-time and well-known mob bookmaker with a history of gambling arrests, had taken on new stature in the Philadelphia–South Jersey underworld.

Morrone, unaware that Perna was wired, contributed to that theory.

"This guy's the biggest fuckin' guy in Jersey," he told Perna as they drove to their first meeting with Sparacio. "He controls the fuckin' bartenders union and everything. . . . That's why I can't fuck up with the guy."

"Right," said Perna.

"You know what I mean?" Morrone said. "Them guys on the phone . . . they just all work for him. . . . He was one of the guys named to take over after Nicky and all."

*   *   *

Nicky was Nicodemo "Little Nicky" Scarfo, the former mob boss of Philadelphia and perhaps the most violent Mafia leader in America. But by October of 1990, the sixty-year-old Scarfo was out of the picture. He had been convicted three different times in the late 1980s for conspiracy, racketeering, and murder. In fact, he was the first organized crime boss since Louie Lepke to be found guilty of first degree murder. And while Scarfo later had that conviction overturned and would be acquitted at his retrial in February 1997, he was still doing time on his federal conspiracy and racketeering convictions, consecutive fourteen- and fifty-five-year terms that guaranteed he would spend the rest of his life behind bars.

Scarfo, a flamboyant gangster's gangster, had ruled the Philadelphia–South Jersey underworld for eight bloody years. Based in Atlantic City, he rode the crest of the casino gambling boom to power, literally shooting his way to the top. He was an arrogant, in-your-face Mafia don, the epitome of the egocentric 1980s, a matching mob bookend for New York's John Gotti.

About thirty gangland killings occurred during the Scarfo era, and about thirty other mobsters were convicted along with him as a result of the investigations that followed.

Sparacio and "Tony Buck" Piccolo, both in their late sixties, were among the few who survived both the carnage and the prosecutorial onslaught. Piccolo, who was Scarfo's cousin, served as acting boss of the crime family briefly in 1989, but the wily old mobster was smart enough to realize the high-profile position came at a heavy price. Scarfo was in jail for life; his two predecessors, Philip Testa and Angelo Bruno, had been murdered.

Tony Buck, a silver-haired gentleman gambler, eschewed the violent, flamboyant style that was the mark of his cousin. Displaying the intelligence and foresight that had kept him out of jail for most of his life, Piccolo looked beyond the power and prestige of being *capo di tutti capi* in Philadelphia. He wanted no part of the top spot. He was happy, however, to support the Sicilian-born John Stanfa, who had returned to Philadelphia in 1990 after sitting out most of the bloody 1980s in federal prison after being convicted of perjury for lying to a grand jury.

Federal authorities were just beginning to put together the pieces of the newly reorganized Philadelphia mob when the gambling investigation began. And while Morrone's boast that his boss was now one of the top guys proved to be an overstatement, it nevertheless led investigators to the very top of the organization.

"All my life, all I ever done was book," Shotsie Sparacio said in a conversation picked up much later in the investigation. Unfortunately for Sparacio, the jury didn't see it quite that way. But he might have been telling the truth.

Eddie O'Hanlon was never roughed up. Morrone's threats might have been just that—threats. Perna, with FBI cash, paid back the debt over several months, usually in increments of $400. It was hardly high finance. Credit card companies would have charged more interest.

What's more, several tapes made by Perna showed Sparacio to be a patient, albeit perplexed, bill collector.

Like Morrone, he couldn't understand how O'Hanlon could bet without the money to cover his action. He said it showed a lack of character. It would have been different, he added, if O'Hanlon had covered some earlier losses, established a track record, so to speak. But to fail to pay the first time you lose, what kind of guy was this? Sparacio asked.

"It's a shame we have to go through this," he said. "That's like stealin'. That's like goin' in your pocket and stealin' your money, you know. . . . A guy like that got no character."

"No, none at all," agreed Morrone.

"You know, a guy loses some serious money, then there's a little mark, that's a different story. But you come up ice cold in the beginning. Nothin'. It's like goin' in your house and burglarizin' your home. It's not right."

Sparacio, who had spent all his life on the streets and who had been a wiseguy for close to forty years, also was flabbergasted that someone going to a university, a place of higher learning, would act that way.

"Shame on him and anything he ever does," he told Morrone and Perna during another meeting. "He's a thief. That's a disgrace. A guy going to college to try to have some character or class. Man oh man, if you go through life like that, it's a disgrace. See, it ain't the money. . . ."

Later, when his world started to come apart, when gambling debts were replaced by vendettas, when he himself received a classic underworld "message"—a dead fish and a bullet left in a box on his doorstep—Sparacio talked again about the lack of honor, loyalty, and character in the people around him.

"There's no brains behind nothin'," he said. "There's nowhere you can turn to make sense out of anything. Before, people mediated things, ironed something out. I don't know where it's gonna lead."

By that point, it *was* the money.

Greed and a grab for power had once again sent the Philadelphia mob careening out of control. A bloody underworld power struggle had erupted. Wanton violence and treachery, long the hallmarks of the organization, had returned. Bodies were dropping in the streets. It was the Scarfo era all over again.

And this time the FBI got it on tape.

The gambling investigation that started with Sparacio and Morrone eventually led to the law office of Salvatore J. Avena at 519 Market Street in downtown Camden. From conversations picked up from the bug in the bakery office, investigators realized Sparacio went to Avena's office to meet with Piccolo and Stanfa. Surveillance of the office confirmed that the three mob leaders were often there at the same time. The feds believed this was more than a coincidence. They also doubted that the mobsters were there solely to discuss legal problems. In September of 1991 they sought and received court authorized approval to plant an electronic listening device in the law office conference room where they believed the mobsters met.

On October 4, FBI agents made a "surreptitious entry" into Avena's second-floor suite of offices "during the early morning hours," according to one government document that described the court-sanctioned break-in. Two weeks later, on October 17, the agents went back in to complete the bugging of the conference room.

By November a listening post had been set up in the basement of the federal courthouse at 400 Market Street, a block away. Eventually prosecutors would seek court approval to expand the bugging to Avena's private office and to several other locations in the second-floor suite. But at first, the agents huddled in a small room in the courthouse basement wondered what it was they were supposed to be listening for.

Federal judges do not randomly approve electronic bugging requests, even when the targets are mobsters. Probable cause has to be established. Add the fact that this was a lawyer's office, and the issue became even more ticklish.

"This was approved at the highest levels," said Maher, the FBI agent coordinating the bugging. "Before we did anything, we had to send it all down to Washington."

And under the terms of the court authorization, the feds had to go back before a US District Court judge every thirty days to renew their application for the bugging. In each renewal request, they had to provide ten-day reports, brief synopses of what the bugging had turned up during the previous month.

Both Maher and Gross, the Assistant US Attorney handling the surveillance, were concerned as the first thirty-day period was drawing to a close early in December.

"We didn't have much," Maher admitted. "Then, after the December third tape, I got a call from one of the agents in the basement. 'We just hit a home run,' he said. Two days later, after the December fifth meeting, he called me again. 'Grand slam,' he said."

On December 3, Stanfa and Piccolo met with Joe Sodano and Joe Licata, two members of the crime family's North Jersey crew. Sodano and Licata worked out of Newark under a doddering mob capo named Blackie Napoli whom they wanted replaced.

"I am here to say that I do not believe that Blackie is mentally capable of handling the position and I think he's aware of it," Sodano told Stanfa and Piccolo. "I said, 'Everyone feels that you should step down, that you should retire.' "

What followed was a long and rambling conversation about violations of mob protocol, about Napoli's inability to get along with people, and about the way La Cosa Nostra had begun to deteriorate. Stanfa, with Sodano, Piccolo, and Licata nodding in agreement, said too many "unqualified" people had become members of the organization. Stanfa said he wanted to change that.

While no specific crimes were discussed during that meeting, what the conversation clearly established to investigators was that John Stanfa was the man in charge. And in case there was any doubt, Stanfa, alternately talking in his fractured and heavily accented English and in his native Sicilian, laid it on the table for Sodano and Licata—and for the FBI.

"We don't want quantity, we want quality," he said.

"Just because a guy, maybe, he is a good earner or this and that, I . . . can't go for that, you know what I mean? . . . Joey, believe me. What I know. What I see. Lot of people, they no even belong near us."

"You're right," Sodano said.

"I don't go for no money, Joey. I no hungry for money . . . because Cosa Nostra, Cosa Nostra it's no for money. Money come after. I no got nothing else to say."

"You're talking clear," said Licata. "There's nothing to talk about. You're talking straight."

But they would all have a lot more to say that day about the troubled state of the American Mafia and some of the people who ran it. A transcript of the conversation ran on for seventy-two pages.

2

FBI Surveillance Tape
December 3, 1991
2:07 P.M.

JOE SODANO: Ego, ego is a dangerous thing . . . if you put
power in the wrong hands.
ANTHONY PICCOLO: You've got problems.
SODANO: You got plenty of problems. And a lot of people,
if you, if they think that they are, they're whole, I've
seen guys got straightened out. . . . they would just.
. . . they change their whole posture. They take on.
. . . their air. Their walk changes. Their demeanor. Before, if you talk to the guy . . . now, they'll look at you
like, "fucking piece of shit. Dare approach me."
PICCOLO: Look who I am! Look who I am!

It is, by almost any measure, the most dysfunctional
Mafia family in America, an organization torn apart by
its own indiscriminate use of violence and lack of self-
discipline.

Since 1980, two of its bosses have been brutally slain
and three others have spent more time in jail than they
have on the streets. Thirty members and associates, including a generation of potential leaders, have been
killed. At least fifty others have been convicted and sentenced to jail terms.

And most troubling of all from an underworld perspective, nearly a dozen members and associates have testified in court, shattering *omertà*, the Mafia's time-honored code of silence and the concepts of honor and loyalty that supposedly went with it.

This is La Cosa Nostra Philadelphia style—a crime family without any recognizable value system, the Simpsons of the Underworld, The Gang that Couldn't Think Straight. Its problematic nature was on display throughout the Stanfa investigation. The case that grew out of that probe painted a picture of widespread underworld incompetence exacerbated by senseless violence. Similar portraits have emerged in mob trials around the country, leading many in law enforcement—and even some sources in the underworld—to proclaim that the American Mafia is dead. An obituary may be premature, but in the last fifteen years, more than 1,200 mob members and associates have been convicted, targeted in multipronged federal attacks that have shaken the once highly secretive and seemingly invincible criminal society.

Mob bosses in most major American cities, including New York, Philadelphia, Chicago, Boston, Pittsburgh, Newark, Cleveland, and Kansas City, have been jailed. Mob-tainted unions have been seized by the government. Mob-controlled industries have been turned inside out.

Mob informants are everywhere.

These "men of honor," who once swore a blood oath to live and die by the gun, now do their swearing from the witness stand while their agents negotiate book deals and peddle movie rights. Now the only people making offers that can't be refused are the authorities who run the Witness Protection Program and the producers who run Hollywood.

"The traditional values have changed," says Patrick J. Ryan, a New York–based professor of criminal justice and former director of the International Association for the Study of Organized Crime. "The value system is different. . . . Seniority used to engender respect. Today it means nothing. . . . Obedience used to be big. Now you see guys disregarding the directives of a boss.

"None of this is mysterious. What's happening is happening in society in general. . . . Cultures change. Societies change. We don't go and kiss our fathers' rings anymore."

There are more than two dozen "made," or formally initiated, members of La Cosa Nostra cooperating with the government today. In testimony in federal courtrooms across America, they have told a spellbinding tale of greed, treachery, violence, and deceit that is at the root of the demise of the American mob.

From Phil Leonetti's cavalier comment about murder—"I never did nothing ruthless besides, well, I would kill people. But that's our life. That's what we do"—to Salvatore Gravano's description of his blind allegiance to his former boss John Gotti—"When he barked, I bit"—the words of these high level informants have mesmerized jurors, filled thousands of pages of court transcripts, and led to long prison sentences for hundreds of American mob figures.

Fifteen years ago, the Justice Department launched an all-out attack on La Cosa Nostra. Taking advantage of high-tech electronic surveillance and the broad and devastating powers of the Racketeering Influenced and Corrupt Organizations (RICO) Act, prosecutors won a series of convictions that ripped away the hierarchy of most major American mob families. According to statistics compiled by the FBI, thirty mob bosses, twelve underbosses, nine consiglières and eighty-two capos (or captains) have been convicted since 1980. The leaders of twenty of America's twenty-five recognized Cosa Nostra families have been jailed, including the bosses of four of the five New York families.

One of the last to fall was Vincent "The Chin" Gigante, head of the Genovese crime family. For years, before his conviction in June 1997, Gigante ducked prosecution by feigning mental illness, walking around Greenwich Village in a bathrobe and slippers, mumbling to himself. Detectives once went to arrest Gigante in his Lower Manhattan home and found him standing in a shower, fully clothed and holding an umbrella.

It is the perfect image for the American Mafia, a once arrogantly macho institution reduced to chicanery to survive. What's more, the organization has been split by a generational and cultural divide not unlike the one that has affected society. Second-and third-generation gangsters, products of middle-class America, make lousy Mafiosi. They value form over substance. They have little sense of history. They assume instant gratification as a birthright. And, time and again they have shown, they cannot deal with adversity.

FBI Agent Joseph Pistone, who infiltrated the Colombo crime family and posed as an aspiring wiseguy for several years in the late 1980s (and later co-wrote the book *Donnie Brasco* about his exploits), told a United States Senate subcommittee that he saw the changes as he worked side-by-side with members of a Colombo crew in New York.

"With each generation the Mafia subculture moves closer to mainstream America," Pistone said in a 1990 appearance before the subcommittee. "The old-timers who exhibit the strongest values of the Mafia are aging and slowly dying off. They are being replaced by younger wiseguys. . . . who do not possess the same strong family values. . . .

"I continually heard the older members complaining about this phenomenon. They were concerned that the new members cared more about themselves than they did about the family or crew. 'Our thing' was turning into 'my thing.' "

Leonetti, Scarfo's nephew and underboss, and Gravano, Gotti's underboss and close friend, are two of the more celebrated Mafia turncoats now testifying for the government. Both are examples of the phenomenon Pistone discussed in Washington.

Reflecting the get-it-all, get-it-now philosophy of the 1980s, Nicky Scarfo in Philadelphia and John Gotti in New York scoffed at tradition in a blatant grab for power and wealth. Both abandoned the patient, plodding, and circumspect style that had been the mark of older, more traditional mob bosses.

They recruited younger members, like Leonetti and Gravano, who became part of the new-look American Mafia. These new Mafiosi took a high profile, grabbing with both fists for expensive homes, fancy cars, and finely tailored clothes. And when things got tough, they traded what they knew to hold onto as much of that wealth as they could.

Gravano admitted his involvement in nineteen Mafia murders. Leonetti claimed ten. Cold-blooded hit men, they now do their shooting from the witness stand, where they have proven to be just as deadly. In exchange they've been set free (each served about five years in prison), given new identities, and relocated somewhere in Middle America.

They top a staggering list of informants who have either disappeared into the federal Witness Protection Program or who are cooling their heels in special protective custody wings located in federal prisons in New York, New Jersey, Minnesota, and Arizona. From the Lucchese family there is former acting boss Alphonse "Little Al" D'Arco, underboss Anthony "Gas Pipe" Casso, and capos Anthony "Tumac" Accetturo and Peter Chiodo. From the Colombo family there is former consiglie're Carmine Sessa, capo and self-styled "Yuppie Don" Michael Franzese and the late Gregory Scarpa. From the Genovese family, there is Vincent "The Fish" Cafaro of New York and Angelo Lonardo of Cleveland. Joining Gravano from the Gambino organization is Dominick "Fat Dom" Borghese.

And then there's what one investigator called the "South Philadelphia Boys' Choir," headed of course by Leonetti and including former capos Thomas DelGiorno and Lawrence Merlino and mob soldiers Nicholas "Nicky Crow" Caramandi, Eugene "Gino" Milano and George Fresolone.

"When the mob was first formed in this country in 1930, it was made up of first generation Italian Americans, either people that were born here or who had come at an early age," said Ronald Goldstock, former director of New York State's Organized Crime Task Force, in a 1988 appearance before the same Senate subcommittee that later heard from Pistone.

"The ties that bound members . . . together were those of honor, kinship, and respect. We are now in the second

and third generation of the mob, and the new members
have grown up differently. They have the values of their
contemporaries. They are the sociological equivalent of
yuppies. Their values are not those of honor and respect;
they are economic. The ties that bind them to the mob
are financial in nature.''

Fred Martens, former executive director of the Pennsylvania Crime Commission, offers a simpler explanation.

"For the older guys, the Mafia was a way of life. For
these younger guys, it's a way to make money.''

Sitting in the basement of the federal courthouse in
downtown Camden, New Jersey, FBI agents monitoring
the conversation of Stanfa, Sodano, Piccolo, and Licata
early in December 1991 heard much the same thing.

SODANO: Guys become crazy. They become crazy. I seen
    it in New York with guys that straightened out their
    sons that are twenty, twenty-two. They're the same
    person they were yesterday. They didn't change over-
    night.
PICCOLO: Sure.
SODANO: If they're gonna get wisdom, they're not gonna
    get it in one day. . . . Takes years. . . . But that's one
    of the major problems of this whole thing. Guys who
    put power in the hands of people (who) are incompe-
    tent. They just don't have the mental capacity.
    They're egomaniacs. They're show-offs. They're
    fuckin' bullies. When they didn't have power. . . .
    Now, they're "Motherfucker. Don't you bring me some
    fuckin' . . . I'll fuckin' cut your. . . . '' They forget who
    they are. They go fuckin' crazy.
PICCOLO: We have the same thing here with all them cow-
    boys. You know that, John? That's what happened
    here.

The investigation had been going slowly up to that point. A special FBI detail had been assigned surveillance outside of Avena's law office, and on several occasions members of the squad had spotted different mobsters entering the building.

Under the terms of the court-authorized bugging operation, federal authorities had to have a reason to turn on their monitoring equipment before they could begin listening. They also had to "minimize" their eavesdropping, close down their monitoring if a conversation had nothing to do with the criminal activities being investigated. There were days when the agents sitting in the basement of the courthouse and those out on the street watching the law office saw and heard nothing. If no one showed up, there was no justifiable reason to activate the microphones.

More frustrating were the days when someone of interest did show up, and the bugs in the conference room picked up nothing. On November 26, 1991, for example, agents watching 519 Market Street saw Stanfa, Piccolo, and Joe Licata enter the building for a meeting that federal authorities had been tipped off about in advance.

The agents in the basement geared up their electronic surveillance equipment. But the bugs in the conference room of Avena's law office picked up nothing but background noises. The mobsters were meeting somewhere other than the room in which the bugs had been planted.

A week later, it appeared the same scenario was about to play out. This time the feds went in for a closer look. Mark Pinero, a stocky, dark-haired Philadelphia police organized crime detective working undercover with the FBI task force, was doing outside surveillance that day and twice boldly entered the law office building.

Avena's suite of eight rooms is on the second floor. The stairs leading to his reception area are just inside the Market Street doorway. At the top of the stairs is another door that opens onto the office suite.

At about 1:30 in the afternoon, Pinero spotted Piccolo walking toward the law office and decided to follow. An FBI affidavit, submitted a month later to support a request to expand the office bugging, details what happened next:

"On arrival at the second floor doorway, Pinero observed that Piccolo was nowhere in view. Pinero noted that the door to Salvatore Avena's office was open and that the conference room was unoccupied. Pinero departed without conversing with anyone in the office."

A half hour later, Stanfa and another man showed up. Pinero again followed them in, boldly posing as a potential client:

Stanfa's companion held the door open so Pinero could enter. Pinero observed that the conference room was still unoccupied, but that the door to Salvatore Avena's office was now closed. On instruction from Stanfa, the receptionist telephoned Avena and informed him that 'John' was there. The receptionist informed Stanfa that Avena would 'be right with you.' Pinero made a brief inquiry of the receptionist and departed.

At 2:07 that afternoon, Licata was spotted entering 519 Market Street. This time Pinero stayed put, but he once again alerted the squad in the courthouse basement. A minute later, Stanfa, Piccolo, Licata, and Joe Sodano sat down for a long talk in the conference room. The investigation that would bring down the Philadelphia mob was up and running. First the mobsters discussed the problem they were having with Blackie Napoli, the capo in Newark whom both Sodano and Licata wanted replaced. Stanfa agreed to go along and Piccolo concurred. Before the afternoon was over, however, federal agents monitoring the conversation had gotten a primer on the sad state of the American Mafia, the wiseguy version of what Pistone and Goldstock brought to the U.S. Senate subcommittee.

STANFA: Joe, I told you. Over here it's . . . believe me. . . . clean it up. That's what you need. That's what you need. . . .

SODANO: I don't know the answer. . . . This last guy [Gravano] that went bad with John Gotti, I'm glad I don't know this guy.

PICCOLO: You don't know him at all, Joe?

SODANO: Never met him. He's a younger guy. I never met him. But I'm sure John must be fucking sick. . . . I know the old guy. I know John pretty good but I know the other guy, Frankie LoCascio [a Gotti capo]. . . . He's a good, solid man, but he brought his own son into it and his son is an example of one of them guys.

PICCOLO: He went the other way.

SODANO: Thinks he's ten feet tall. And John, his son is a young man. You, first of all, it's an insult to people who are knowledgeable, who have been around you for twenty-five, thirty, forty years. His son, he may be your blood, he may be ready . . . but it's more than that.

PICCOLO: That's right.

SODANO: Does he have the ability to guide people? Can he keep people out of trouble? Create justice? And . . . create money? Or is he just going to create havoc, bedlam?

PICCOLO: That's what happens.

SODANO: How many young men are capable of having

good judgment? It's impossible. You've got to live the
years. . . . There are so many things that are . . . I
don't know how to straighten them out. I don't know
how to straighten them out.

STANFA: Joe, I wish, I wish I knew. I admit it.

SODANO: Here. A guy like Tommy Del [Thomas Del-
Giorno]. He was a good man. He never should have
been straightened out.

STANFA: No.

SODANO: But he should have been a bookmaker. Period.

STANFA: Joe, between us . . . this other guy became part
a problem from the first day, Shotsie. He don't know
nothing from nothing. Joe, I'm up to here, Joe, I can't
take Shotsie. . . . He don't belong. . . . When I came
into this thing, it's good. You know what we do. He
said, we put Tony boss. He say, "I'll be the underboss," he appoint himself. He said, "You gonna be consigliere." I say. "What, what are you talking about?"
. . . This guy, they no even know what the fuck he is,
what day is. . . . See, where I come from Joe, somebody talk to you that way, they no even, they no even
walk from the fucking room. Okay? Hey, over there, I
know. It's forget about it. . . .

SODANO: You see, if things are done right, it's all good
men.

STANFA: I know.

SODANO: So, whoever you take is a good man. But when
you got a lot of shit inside. . . .

(Later)

STANFA: Now . . . believe me. Like I told you, it's most of
the people, they want to be in this because they're
thinking that . . . tough people. They go over there,
"Hey, you give me so much money."

SODANO: And then most of them have never been tested.

STANFA: No. That's it. That's it.

PICCOLO: That's the story, Joe.

SODANO: I, I don't know the answer . . . because the
problems are the same in Newark. They're the
same. . . .

PICCOLO: All over.

SODANO: . . . in New York.

PICCOLO: All over.

SODANO: In Brooklyn. . . . They're bad problems.

STANFA: I don't look at this way, because I figure this way. . . . See, you see somebody, they jumpin' from the window. Because they gotta jump, I gotta jump, too?

SODANO: I feel the same way. I don't care what other people do. I'm not gonna change my principles. Not one bit. . . . I don't give a fuck. Whatever happens, happens. I don't give a fuck. But you have to remember, that they're not too many people that think that way. Not too many.

STANFA: Yeah.

SODANO: The RICO problem. Thirty years, twenty years for each count. When they give you forty, fifty, sixty, there are not many people who can handle it.

PICCOLO: That's right.

SODANO: They just can't handle it. We may be in an era, unless you take your son and you raise him, if you feel he's meant for that life, and you raise him yourself and his sons or his nephews, or his grandson, and you go through, like if you had them in Italy or in Sicily, and you just keep them and you raise them, if they're inclined, if they have that mind. But otherwise . . .

PICCOLO: Forget about it.

SODANO: You don't know. You don't really know what people's motives are. In fact, most people don't have the same motives that you have. It's this. It's showing off. It's . . . and John Gotti. He's a good man, John, but he allowed himself to get caught up where . . . well, he became on the front page of magazines and newspapers. He made it easy for them.

STANFA: Yeah.

PICCOLO: Sure.

SODANO: How about he made everybody come and see him. Cameras. TVs. This. That. They know everybody. Those guys that were, nobody ever heard of these

guys. . . . I never heard of them in my fucking life.
They were in their seventies. That's the way it's supposed to be.

PICCOLO: Sure.

SODANO: But no more. There's no more hidden people.
There's no hidden.

PICCOLO: They're in the open.

SODANO; Isn't it a good thing you could be in Mafia, right,
but nobody knows it? I can do a lot of things for you.

STANFA: Joey.

SODANO: If nobody knows.

STANFA: I feel that.

PICCOLO: That's right.

STANFA: You know, one time, old man told me, "John,
see over here?" He say, "The police, they put their
name, who they are, and what they work." Listen.
They're not supposed to know who we are.

PICCOLO: That's right. That's right.

(*Later*)

SODANO: Anyway, you know, I think probably, some of
the best guys for this kind of life are guys that are
criminals. They're thieves. They stole out of necessity.
They were criminals. They were always against the
law. Other people, come into it, they want to come in
with a suit and a tie and thirty pounds overweight.
And then pose. And they never were against the law.
They never got kicked in the balls.

STANFA: Joe.

SODANO: They never, it's just, they're not ready for it.

STANFA: Believe me, it's a shame. . . . Me, I don't change
a bit. What I was do before, I keep on doing. Every
single morning, you see me, you know, around seven-
thirty, I leave from my house. I drop my daughter. I
go to work. I'm here because I got to be here. In other
words, I'm there working.

PICCOLO: That's right.

STANFA: You know what I mean? But, some people, like
you say, they want to be with the suit and tie. They
want to be, you know, look like . . .

PICCOLO: Nineteen sixty-five it was like this. Right. I

thought of him. He belonged to that guy. Now I'm talking about people, don't misunderstand me, but if I went . . . I told Angelo]Bruno[. I went out and I said, "Listen, I'm gonna go to work. . . . You need me, you call whenever you need me. You call." So I went to work. Started my own business.

SODANO: I can understand that.

PICCOLO: And I work, like seven to eight, but whenever they had . . . getting back to what you said before. I wasn't worried about this and about that. Get the . . . if you need me, you call me. I'm available to you. And the same with my cousin [Scarfo]. I mean, forget about all the mistakes that were made. Forget about everything, Joe. Cause I don't even want to think about it sometimes.

SODANO: I can imagine.

PICCOLO: But I didn't want to be with ten people. . . . You got this guy [Scarfo], when he started, when he went away and he came back and when he did that bit for the gun, came back. I told him, I said, "You got a bunch of cowboys. They're gonna put you in jail. Or they're gonna kick you in the butt." "Ah, don't worry. I'll take care them." "Okay, if you need me, call me."

It was more gossip than evidence, but it was startling. Here were wiseguys completely at ease, talking at length about " the life."

It was, indeed, a home run for Jim Maher and the rest of the FBI. It was a classic overview, a saga—the kind of tape you'd play for the jury at the opening of a trial. *Sit and listen. Here is what it's all about. Pay attention. This is not us telling you. This is the way it really is. There are the defendants, over there at the defense table. And here are their words. What more needs to be said?*

Once that tape was transcribed, the feds felt confident they'd win another thirty-day extension for the bug in Avena's conference room. What they got two days later was even better.

3

John Stanfa was the guy who was going to put it all back together. That was the conventional wisdom in law enforcement and underworld circles when the balding, broad-shouldered, forty-nine-year-old former bricklayer surfaced as Philadelphia's new mob boss in 1990.

He had been born and raised in Sicily, schooled in the ways of La Cosa Nostra. Some even said he had been "made" there before emigrating to the United States in 1964. He had done time in prison—more than six years of an eight-year sentence for perjury—without opening his mouth, another sign that he understood what it meant to do the right thing; that he embraced *omertà* which, literally translated, means "to be a man."

A 1991 Pennsylvania Crime Commission report, noting Stanfa's new status, warned of his "national and international organized crime connections' and suggested that the "older values and traditions" of the Sicilian Mafia that he embodied would "regenerate an ailing American La Cosa Nostra." With one foot in Sicily and the other in the United States, Stanfa was portrayed as the prototype of the new American mob boss. More Angelo Bruno than Nicky Scarfo, more Carlo Gambino than John Gotti, he was described as the per-

36

fect leader for a mob family wracked by years of violence, prosecution, and turncoat testimony. Now, the pundits in law enforcement and media circles predicted, the mob would go back to the old ways. Now, it was said, the wiseguys would be more interested in making money than in making headlines.

This proved to be a gross overstatement. As it turned out, Stanfa was more Scarfo than Bruno. He just hid it with a thick Sicilian accent that made him seem wily and circumspect. The conversations picked up in Avena's office over the next two years would show all that. What also emerged was an arrogance that had only been hinted at in the past.

Stanfa was a Mafia snob.

He thought little of his American brethren. "Over here, it's like kindergarten," he said in one telling conversation. During the mob war that raged in 1993, he repeatedly referred to his young rivals as the "little Americans," and, in a favorite Sicilian epithet, called them "cuckolds."

"They can't even shine our shoes," he would say, searching for the right English phrase to belittle them.

John Stanfa was born on December 7, 1940, in the tiny mountain village of Caccamo, about thirty miles southeast of Palermo, in a region of western Sicily long dominated by the Mafia. The youngest of four children, Stanfa has two older brothers and a brother-in-law who have been identified by Italian and American law enforcement authorities as members of the Sicilian mob. Another relative, Antonio Guiffre, a nephew through marriage, was the local mob boss, according to Italian law enforcement authorities.

Shortly after coming to America, Stanfa married Ni-
colena Congialdi, a young woman from his village who
had also come to the States. They moved to Philadelphia, an area where Lena already had relatives. In 1967,
their first child, Sara, was born. A son, Joseph, came
four years later. And in 1976, just before all the trouble
started, another daughter, Maria, was born.

Based on information later supplied by mob informants, federal authorities have pieced together a sketch of
Stanfa's early years in the Philadelphia mob. A bricklayer and stonemason by trade, he came to the city with
an introduction from Carlo Gambino, New York's boss
of bosses and a close personal friend of Angelo Bruno,
the longtime Mafia don in the City of Brotherly Love.
Gambino asked Bruno to find a spot for Stanfa as a favor
to some Sicilian mob figures who were friends of his.

Stanfa's connections to the Gambino family in New
York and to powerful Mafia forces in Palermo would
later save his life and set the stage for his rise to power
in Philadelphia. But in the late 1960s in the relative quiet
of the Bruno underworld, his arrival went largely unnoticed. For years, in fact, local authorities were not
even aware that Stanfa had become a made member of
the Bruno organization. He was thought to be little more
than a mob associate, a stonemason who lived with his
family in a modest, brick rowhouse on Passyunk Avenue
and who was spotted occasionally hanging around with
wiseguys.

That quiet, unassuming lifestyle reflected the Bruno
image.

An avuncular man who took a decidedly low profile,
Angelo Bruno lived several blocks from Stanfa in a
three-story brownstone near Tenth Street and Snyder

Avenue in the heart of South Philadelphia. The mob boss dressed in nondescript business suits bought off the rack at local department stores and rode around town in Plymouths and Chevys. He avoided the limelight and generally got along with everyone, even those who had been investigating him for years.

Jim Maher, the FBI agent who later supervised the Stanfa probe, tells a story about the time he and another young agent went to Bruno's home on Snyder Avenue to serve him with a subpoena. Maher said Bruno's wife, Susan, was beside herself with worry when the agents announced themselves and asked to be let into the home. Sobbing and wringing her hands, she made a great show of her concern, Maher said.

"Bruno was upstairs in his underwear, shaving," Maher recalled. "He called down the steps and told his wife to send us up. So we went up and handed him the subpoena."

Then, in typical fashion, Bruno put the whole incident in perspective.

"You'll have to excuse my wife," he told Maher. "She takes these things seriously."

Bruno's rap sheet included several arrests for gambling and bookmaking, but the only serious time he ever did in prison was a two-year stint for contempt in the early 1970s, after he refused to testify at an organized crime hearing being conducted by the New Jersey State Commission of Investigation. He listed his occupation as "salesman' for a local vending machine company— a company that, to no one's surprise, saw its business boom in Atlantic City shortly after the 1976 casino gambling referendum in which voters legalized Boardwalk gaming palaces. At the time of his death four years later, he was said to be worth millions, with secret real estate holdings in Florida, hidden interests in foreign casinos, and a massive stock portfolio.

Violence, which later became the calling card of the Philadelphia Mafia, was a negotiating tool of last resort for Bruno, who nonetheless recognized that murder was sometimes necessary in the business in which he made his mark. People were killed during Bruno's twenty-one-year reign as mob boss, but their deaths were seldom trumpeted in newspaper headlines. More often than not, someone who had crossed Bruno and who had rejected his offers at compromise and reconciliation would simply disappear. In Sicily, they called it the "white death."

One story about a murder ordered by Bruno tells you all you need to know about the old Mafia kingpin. This happened in the early 1960s. The victim had apparently been robbing bookmakers connected to the organization and had ignored warnings to stop.

Nicky Scarfo, then a mob soldier, got the hit contract. The victim was lured to a bar in southern New Jersey, where he was strangled and stabbed to death. According to a plan laid out by Bruno, Scarfo's murder crew then took the body to a spot in the woods nearby where another Bruno crew had already dug a grave. But Scarfo and his henchmen were told not to bury the body. Their instructions were to simply leave it next to the neatly dug hole. Another crew, they were told, would take care of the final arrangements.

What happened next, say law enforcement authorities, was classic Bruno.

Two men whom Bruno trusted were sent to retrieve the body. First they filled in the grave with dirt. Then they took the victim and buried him at another location.

That way, if any member of Scarfo's crew or the crew originally assigned to dig the grave decided to inform, they'd have nothing to deliver. Anyone who went to the original grave site would dig up an empty hole.

Investigators contrast that story with a hit carried out on Scarfo's orders several years later.

In August 1982, a Scarfo hit man shot and wounded the father of a mob informant in the office of a Wildwood Crest motel. The hit man was wearing a ski mask and an expensive designer sweatsuit. The shooting, the first time an "innocent" family member had been targeted for mob retribution, was considered a seminal event in the deterioration of "mob values." Family members—the sons, parents, brothers, or nephews of mob figures at war with one another—had long been considered protected by an unwritten code of conduct. Much would be made of this a few years later, when the sister of New York mob informant Peter Chiodo was gunned down in Brooklyn, but it was Scarfo who first thumbed his nose at that mob protocol.

More to the point, however, was what happened the day after that shooting in Wildwood Crest. Law enforcement investigators watching Scarfo's home and office in Atlantic City saw the mob boss and two top associates boldly walking the streets in the same type of designer sweatsuit the hit man had worn the night before. Unlike Bruno, Scarfo wanted to attract attention to himself.

Angelo Bruno was killed on March 21, 1980, at around 9:45 P.M., in front of his home on Snyder Avenue. His assassin walked up from behind the car in which Bruno was sitting on that rainy night, took a double-barreled shotgun from under his raincoat, leveled it at the back of Bruno's head, and pulled the trigger.

Bruno was sitting in the passenger seat of a maroon 1979 Chevy Caprice Classic. Depending on whose version of events is to be believed, the passenger side window was either already down, or the driver of the car, seeing the gunman approach in the rearview mirror, hit the electronic button on his door panel and lowered the window, setting Bruno up for the kill.

The man behind the wheel that night was John Stanfa. He was slightly wounded. Several shotgun pellets grazed his arm. Taken to the hospital and later questioned by authorities, he said he knew nothing about the biggest gangland hit in Philadelphia history. Three days later, he was spotted traveling to Newark and New York with three mobsters suspected of orchestrating the Bruno murder. FBI surveillance photos later shown to a grand jury investigating Bruno's murder showed Stanfa getting into a car in South Philadelphia with Frank Sindone, a major mob loan shark. Another picture showed Stanfa and Sindone in front of the 311 Club in Newark with Bruno's consiglière, Antonio "Tony Bananas" Caponigro. FBI agents later tailed the mobsters to the Skyline Motel on Forty-ninth Street in Manhattan, where they met with members of the Genovese organization.

Until the Avena tapes, the only Stanfa comments that made the public record came during his grand jury testimony in 1980, testimony for which he was later convicted of perjury.

On March 31, 1980, he made his first appearance before that investigative panel. One of the prosecutors questioning him was Joel Friedman, a Deputy US Attorney and head of the Organized Crime Strike Force.

(Fifteen years later, Friedman headed the prosecution team that convicted Stanfa.)

Stanfa admitted that he had been visited in the hospital after the Bruno shooting by Sindone and John "Johnnie Keys" Simone, another local mobster. But he offered little about what was discussed. A policeman assigned to guard Stanfa's hospital room had reported the visit, but said that because Sindone and Simone spoke to Stanfa in Italian, he did not know what was said.

"I see an Italian guy, I prefer to talk Italian because my English is not so good," Stanfa explained to the grand jury.

Stanfa also said he knew nothing about the shooting, emphasizing that if he did, he would readily tell authorities.

"I was close with Mister Bruno," he said. "I respect him like I respect my own father. See, I see someone, I was glad to tell you people to stop them more. . . . It was ridiculous. Mister Bruno never deserved that."

Stanfa was ordered to come back for a second round of questioning on April 21. Three days before that session, police in New York discovered the bodies of Caponigro and Alfred "Freddy" Salerno, Caponigro's brother-in-law, in the trunks of two cars abandoned in the South Bronx. Both mobsters had been brutally beaten and tortured. Caponigro had twenty-dollar bills stuffed into his mouth and anus, an underworld sign that he had been killed because he had gotten greedy. Years later, mob informants explained to authorities that Caponigro had orchestrated the Bruno murder because he was convinced Bruno had gotten too old and set in his ways and, as a result, was missing an opportunity to cash in on the casino gambling boom in Atlantic City and the lucrative drug trade that had begun to flourish all over the country. Members of the Genovese family—in a double-cross of Machiavellian proportions—had led Caponigro to believe the Bruno hit was sanctioned by the Mafia Commission in New York. In fact, the Genovese organization wanted both Bruno and Caponigro out of the way so their members could move more easily in Atlantic City and so they could gain control of a $2 million Jersey City bookmaking operation run by Caponigro.

"Tony [Caponigro] went to New York thinking they were gonna make him boss," mob informant Nicholas "Nicky Crow" Caramandi later explained. "Instead, they killed him."

So it was a clearly nervous and agitated John Stanfa who showed up for his grand jury appearance on April 21. Again, however, he said very little. He described himself as a "working man" and continued to insist that he knew nothing about the Bruno murder. If he had seen the gunman approaching, he told the grand jury in his fractured English, "I can push the gas in the car and take off with Mister Bruno. You know what I mean? If I see somebody coming. I don't see nobody coming. We was just talking, side-by-side. And all at once, I hear the explosion. That's the way I see."

He said he knew about shotguns because his favorite sport was "hunting." But he said he had few other interests or vices.

"I never touch drugs," he said. "I don't believe in that.

"I no gamble. I don't go, in other words, sit in a bar or drink. My favorite sport is hunting. . . . My family come first before any sports or anything, because I want to make sure my family got food on the table.''

Asked if Frank Sindone, then a prime target of the Bruno murder investigation, had ever given him any money, he said, ''I wish he does because I told you right now, I got a hole in my pocket. I don't work all winter and now this. . . .''

During that second appearance, a grand juror asked Stanfa when he became an American citizen. Stanfa said he thought it was in 1967 or 1968. Records now indicate it was in 1972.

The juror then asked who were his witnesses at the naturalization ceremony.

''I don't remember who was there,'' he said.

''I guess it wasn't a very memorable occasion if you don't remember the people that were the witnesses,'' said the juror.

Stanfa also said he didn't remember or couldn't recall trips to Newark and New York with Sindone and Caponigro days after Bruno was killed, the perjury for which he was later convicted. And once again he praised the fallen mob boss.

''As a matter of fact,'' he told the grand jury, ''[Bruno's] wife looked at me, like I was, you know, her son. Closer to my wife, the kids, you know. I tell the truth. It was really a disgrace because that guy never deserved that. He was really a gentleman. I don't think nobody can be, you know, in his place, can be the same and be no better. He have so much class. Unbelievable.''

Unbelievable was also the word the grand jury applied to Stanfa's testimony.

He was indicted for perjury on May 14, 1980. But by that point, he had disappeared. Some people in law enforcement suspected that, like Caponigro and Salerno, he was dead. In September, the bullet-riddled body of Johnnie Keys Simone was found near a landfill in Staten Island. In October, Frank Sindone turned up dead in a trash bag behind a variety store in South Philadelphia. While federal authorities never solved the Bruno murder—perhaps ''never brought anyone to trial for the killing'' is a better way to phrase it—most law enforcement and underworld sources say those responsible were brought to justice. It was capital punishment, Mafia-style.

Only John Stanfa survived.

On December 11 he was arrested outside an apartment complex in Lanham, Maryland, a Washington, DC, suburb. He was using the alias Frank DeMario and driving a car registered to a construction company linked to associates of the Gambino crime family. He also used the name Frank Valenti and had another identification in the name of Filippo Davorio of 1922 Twenty-first Street in Brooklyn. Stanfa was working as chef and manager of a restaurant/pizza shop in a mall in Landover, Maryland. The restaurant was also said to be tied to members of the Gambino organization.

For about eight months, Stanfa, who had grown a mustache and goatee, lived in hiding, leaving his wife and three young children back in Philadelphia where, Stanfa's lawyer later said in court, they had been subsisting on food stamps after depleting the family savings.

Stanfa, meanwhile—the man who had told the grand jury his most important concern was seeing that his family had food on the table—was living with a girlfriend from the Philadelphia area who had gone into hiding with him. It was the girlfriend's car, a 1979 white Cadillac with Pennsylvania tags, that had led investigators to the Forest Lake Apartments where, police believed, she and Stanfa had set up house that summer.

The apartment complex was located on Good Luck Road.

FBI agents who collared Stanfa that morning found a decidedly different mobster than the one who had politely and naively answered questions before the grand jury in Philadelphia. When one asked him pointedly why he had gone to New York with Sindone and Caponigro after Bruno was killed, Stanfa replied, "To get a cup of coffee. . . . It's a free country, isn't it?"

On April 21, 1981, Stanfa was sentenced to eight years in prison for lying to the grand jury. That was one month after Bruno's successor, Philip Testa, was killed in a brutal bomb blast that rocked his South Philadelphia neighborhood. Testa's ally, close friend and consigliere, Nicodemo "Little Nicky" Scarfo, assumed the top spot in the organization, setting the stage for a bloody power struggle that would forever change the face of La Cosa Nostra in Philadelphia.

By the time Scarfo was jailed in 1987, the crime family was in shambles. Honor and loyalty had been replaced by treachery and deceit. Any problem, no matter how small, was dealt with through the barrel of the gun. Nick Caramandi and Tommy DelGiorno, convinced that Scarfo planned to have them killed, had run to the feds in 1986, the first in a long line of mob informants who would turn the organization inside out.

A series of successful prosecutions, with DelGiorno and Caramandi as the key government witnesses, followed.

Stanfa was released from prison in April 1987, at

about the same time Scarfo and most of the top members of his organization were being sentenced to lengthy prison terms. The former bricklayer, now balding and barrel-chested, kept a low profile for the next several years. Law enforcement authorities believe he spent some time in Sicily and in New York City before returning to Philadelphia in late 1989 or early in 1990. At that point, Anthony Piccolo was a reluctant acting boss anxious to step aside for younger blood.

Stanfa, with Piccolo's backing and the approval of the Gambino and Genovese crime families in New York, took the top spot. Piccolo became consiglière. Eventually Joseph Ciancaglini Jr., the thirty-three-year-old son of a Scarfo crime family capo jailed on racketeering charges, was named underboss.

In an affidavit submitted with the first request for authorization to bug Avena's Camden law office, Maher had outlined Stanfa's suspected role in the Bruno killing and how federal authorities believed he survived the bloody retribution that followed.

Maher said former New York mob boss Paul Castellano, who headed the Gambino family in 1980, had interceded, convincing Testa and Scarfo to call off a murder contract they had placed on Stanfa shortly before he went away on the perjury charge.

"Castellano explained that Stanfa had relatives in the Gambino LCN [La Cosa Nostra] family," Maher said in the affidavit, quoting from mob informants familiar with events at that time. "Castellano asked that Stanfa be permitted to live, provided he returned to Sicily after his release from prison."

Later, John Gotti, who killed and succeeded Castellano, asked Scarfo to allow Stanfa to remain in the

United States when his prison term expired. Scarfo, according to Phil Leonetti, agreed. Leonetti told Maher he was present at a meeting between Scarfo and Gotti where that agreement was discussed.

"Leonetti told me that John Stanfa is a fully-initiated member of the LCN, having been inducted into the Philadelphia Family by Angelo Bruno," Maher said. "He said that Stanfa is closely allied with the New York Gambino LCN Family."

It was an alliance that had saved Stanfa's life and that now had him sitting atop the Philadelphia underworld. As FBI agents prepared to monitor the second major mob confab in Avena's conference room that cold December afternoon in 1991, John Stanfa was clearly the man in charge.

4

FBI Surveillance Tape
December 5, 1991
12:54 P.M.

SALVATORE PROFACI: You know, to me, Cosa Nostra's
  very sacred. Okay, and my word is better than anything else that I got to offer.

ANTHONY PICCOLO: That's all you got, Sal.

PROFACI: And if I say something to somebody, if I can't
  deliver, then . . .

PICCOLO: It hurts.

PROFACI: . . . . I can't sleep. . . . That's why I never commit myself, unless I know that I possess . . . what I
  gotta deliver.

JOHN STANFA: Yeah.

PROFACI: And when I got it in my hand, then I'll say, oh,
  let's see if I could do it. . . . But I know I already got it
  . . . but you see, the thing is this. They can't have it
  both ways.

PICCOLO: Can't do it.

PROFACI: They can't have it and respect Cosa Nostra.

The bugging at 519 Market Street was one of the long-
est and most expensive eavesdropping operations ever
undertaken by the FBI. It also was one of the best. The
information gathered in Sal Avena's law office was bet-

ter than that picked up at John Gotti's Ravenite Social
Club on Mulberry Street in Manhattan's Little Italy, or
the intelligence gathered from the listening devices
planted in the palatial residence of the late Paul Castellano on Staten Island. Those were important and helped
make major cases, but the Avena tapes took investigators
to another level.

This was an unprecedented look at the way wiseguys
interact, an unguarded account of how, where, and why
they do business. For 435 days, at a cost of $517,673,
the FBI was a fly on the wall.

The obvious result was the sweeping racketeering indictment that brought down the Stanfa organization. But
the impact of the bugging went beyond the Philadelphia–South Jersey area that Stanfa controlled. What the
feds established when they wired Avena's office was an
underworld listening post. What they got was enough to
open investigations into at least three of New York's
organized crime families.

There were tantalizing details about the mob's influence in the waste hauling/trash disposal business, a multimillion-dollar industry long dominated by the Gambino
and Genovese organizations. And there was a stunning
insider's account of the bloody, internecine power struggle that was wracking the Colombo family.

In fact, excerpts from the December 5, 1991, tape in
which Stanfa and Piccolo met with Salvatore Profaci, a
highly regarded capo in the Colombo organization, were
used in federal racketeering trials in Trenton and Brooklyn more than a year before Stanfa went on trial in Philadelphia. Those cases involved murder charges
connected to the Colombo war.

The powerfully built Profaci, a tough talking but well-spoken Mafia diplomat, dominated the December 5 conversation.

First he went on at length about a dispute between Salvatore Avena and Carmine Franco, partners in AAA Waste Hauling, a Philadelphia-based trash business in which, it was said, the Genovese crime family had a hidden interest. Profaci explained that Avena had invited Franco in as his business partner in a New Jersey trash hauling company about five years earlier and that the two then went into business in Philadelphia as well. But he said Franco was taking advantage of Avena. The New Jersey business had been forced into bankruptcy. Debts were mounting. Avena was being held accountable.

But Franco, Profaci said, didn't care.

"He comes over here, he sees all these beautiful, beautiful opportunities and he starts feeding himself like a pig, okay?" Profaci told Stanfa and Piccolo. "In the meantime, the New Jersey business goes down, goes down, goes down . . . don't pay no attention to the New Jersey business."

Profaci said money disappeared. Different individuals, he said, had absconded with hundreds of thousands of dollars in cash. Still, he said, Franco appeared not to care.

"Today, I got documented where this son of a bitch, over two and a half million dollars that he misappropriated," Profaci said. "I don't want to say 'stole.' "

Now, Profaci said, he and leaders of the Genovese organization had begun discussing a buyout. Either Avena would buy out Franco or Franco would buy out Avena:

"I says, 'Hey, we're in the courts of Philadelphia.' I says, 'We stand a better chance in the courts . . . than anybody.' . . . He says, 'Well we can't let that happen.'

" 'Fine,' I says, 'then you tell Carmine Franco to go sell one of his, uh, Rolls Royces, go bring the money he's stealing and cover the shortfall.' 'Sal,' he says, 'what is it going to take for you to get out?' "

That would be a question that the FBI agents monitoring the bugs in Avena's office would hear debated for months to come.

Profaci, who described Franco as a top moneymaker for the Genovese crime family, said he had been sent down to try to settle the dispute. He alluded to an earlier meeting in New York with the Genovese family, and then said that it appeared to him that Franco and his mob backers were trying to push Avena out of the company and establish a toehold in the Philadelphia area for their organization.

The dispute would come up again and again in a series of tapes made over the next year, with Profaci emphasizing that the problem ought to be resolved in the "court of honor" rather than the "court of law." There was serious concern in underworld circles that the bankruptcy proceeding and a possible civil suit—and the public record they would create—would expose the mob's hidden and highly lucrative interest in the trash hauling business. Profaci said he didn't want to see Avena cheated, but he also said it was important to quietly end the litigation. Otherwise, he implied, Avena's life could be in jeopardy.

"I'm trying to keep us alive, that's what I'm trying to do," Profaci would say in a heated discussion with Avena.

Eventually, Profaci would be joined by mob leader Billy D'Elia from Scranton and by Stanfa and Piccolo in pressuring Avena to accept a two million dollar out-of-court settlement. The issue was not justice. The issue was not Avena's rights. The issue was keeping the dispute private and out of the public eye.

Profaci's interest in helping Avena was familial as well as financial. His son, Joseph, was married to Avena's daughter. Sal Profaci and Sal Avena were in-laws and friends. At that first meeting, Profaci told Piccolo and Stanfa he was upset at the way Avena was being treated by Franco, but not surprised.

"My grandfather, when I was a little boy (told me), 'Salvatore, when strength and reason oppose each other, strength will win and reason becomes worthless.' "

Later, he added that, "they have screwed this man [Avena] . . . so many ways and he don't deserve it." From there he went into great detail, outlining the history of the dispute and the mob players involved in the action. If the feds listening a block away had been able to ask questions, they couldn't have gotten a better debriefing on the mob's role in the garbage business. And it was coming right out of the mouth of a highly regarded and well-connected capo from one of New York's top mob families.

It was an unexpected windfall, the first clear indication of what this investigation might deliver.

PROFACI: Ya know, you invite somebody down, to come to your house, to your business, and all of a sudden . . .

PICCOLO: They gonna eat your shoulders.

PROFACI: He takes over your house and throws you out of your business.

PICCOLO: Jesus Christ almighty.

PROFACI: Last Christmas . . . was the worst. That's when they threw Sal's son [John Avena] out and he [Franco] called over here and he says, you and your fuckin' son stay off of the place. . . . My son, Joe, and myself, I says, "Let's go clip this guy."

PICCOLO: Certainly. Sure.

PROFACI: Clip him. Fuck him.

PICCOLO: That's it. And we would.

PROFACI: That, that was a mistake. . . . We shoulda took him then.

PICCOLO: Right then and there. I wish you'd a told me. . . .

PROFACI: You understand. Because this guy, what right does he got to throw out Sal's son? Sal's a fifty percent partner. Then he . . . then he turned a phony. He says you and your fuckin' son . . . Sal [Avena], that's all he talks about. "Threw my son out. Threw my son out."

PICCOLO: Sure. It hurts.

PROFACI: "Threw my son out. . . . Threw my son out. How do I look in front of my son?" . . . [I say] "Sal. Sal. Patience. We gotta teach these young guys patience, but you gotta have patience."

PICCOLO: We gotta have patience first, sure.

STANFA: Now, what. . . . we wait for?

PROFACI: As of last Tuesday . . . a week before Tuesday, when we were all together, this was what was discussed. One of the items . . . discussed was that Mickey Damino, we got word Mickey Damino was put in charge of this problem.

PICCOLO: Okay.

PROFACI: Evidently, Mickey Damino is now running the family.

PICCOLO: Yeah. For The Chin.

PROFACI: The Chin. You know, so I been waitin', actually, you know we had some serious problems up there.

PICCOLO: Sure you have.

PROFACI: And I don't wanna press business.

PICCOLO: No. No. . . . Go back to the patience, again.

PROFACI: Exactly. . . . Gotta have some conscience.

Gotta have some kind of moral, moral . . . I mean,
what are we, we getting. We getting, I mean, we going
worse than the dogs.
PICCOLO: Worse.
PROFACI: When you don't respect me, I don't respect you.
. . . We don't respect each other. What the hell's the
point?

The dispute over the trash business outlined by Profaci was cited one month later in an affidavit submitted
by Maher in support of an application to expand the
bugging in Avena's office.

Citing information provided earlier by mob informant
Philip Leonetti, Maher described the mob's alleged take-
over of Avena's AAA Waste Disposal Corporation as a
classic example of organized crime's infiltration of a legitimate business.

One of the ways the mob "accumulates power and
wealth is by infiltration of legitimate businesses," Maher
wrote. "[Leonetti] said that this is done by the LCN's
taking advantage of a situation in which the legitimate
businessman needs help and, having nearly nowhere else
to turn, turns to the LCN. In the future, the LCN will
recall that debt and eventually will eliminate the business, either through guile or intimidation or a combi-
nation thereof. Leonetti said that a businessman in hard
times who seeks either financial or managerial help from
LCN members would be thus ensnared."

Leonetti told Maher that Avena had that kind of relationship with the mob in the trash business and that
"any dispute involving the LCN would be resolved . . .
without consideration of Avena." He also said that "the
willingness of the LCN to use violence, even to murder,

gave it a competitive edge in these types of business disputes.''

Avena was in bankruptcy court and was considering a lawsuit, but the feds believed he had gone to Profaci, Stanfa, and Piccolo for help because he was worried about Franco's mob backing and wanted to match strength with strength.

In a comment that encapsulated the feds' jaded view of Avena, Maher noted that, ''In a lawsuit, Avena may prevail, yet he opts for a resolution from the enterprise, the LCN.''

In January 1992 a federal court approved a second break-in at Avena's law office. This time the feds planted a bug in Avena's private office. Now any mob discussion there or in the conference room could be monitored and recorded by the FBI.

''From this conversation,'' Maher wrote of the December 5 taping, ''it is clear that Franco, being aligned with the Genovese LCN Family, is having his interests looked out for by that Family. Avena is being represented in this dispute by the Colombo LCN Family, of which Profaci claimed to be a member.'' Maher said Mickey Damino was a nickname or alias for Michael Generoso, who federal authorities said was running the Genovese crime family at the time for Vincent Gigante.

Profaci was confident Avena would prevail if the issue went to court, but he emphasized that was not to be. He also was concerned that the Genovese family might try to reach a more permanent and deadly settlement of the dispute.

PROFACI:We're all walking on eggs. But, God forbid, something happens. I mean, I, I tell Sal, "Sal, I can't

be with you every minute of the day.'' We are not dealing with honorable people.

STANFA: Yeah.

PICCOLO: That's bad.

PROFACI: So, more than that, I can't tell ya. So, he [Av-
ena] tells me, do I have a right to defend my license?
Do I have a right to defend my person?

PICCOLO: Sure. Where's he go?

PROFACI: So I said, "How could I tell you don't defend
your license."

PICCOLO: That's right.

PROFACI: Forty years you been a lawyer, you gonna jeop-
ardize everything you got because these people don't
give a damn for nobody.

PICCOLO: See, in other words John, if Sal was to go to
court, he would win this thing with hands down. But
what they did is brazen.

STANFA: Yeah. I know. I know.

PICCOLO: But you don't want to come to that.

STANFA: See, what he do, he do the right thing. He try,
in other words, to sit down and talk this thing and
settle their problem. But it look like they don't want
. . . you know what I mean. In other words, they try
to push this guy more and more. . . .

PROFACI: He's in the soup now because, you see, once
they, once when they refused . . . when the judge refused to allow Sal to work out his own differences . . .
that is the beginning of big time trouble.

PICCOLO: Sure.

PROFACI: Why, because now the court gonna appoint
somebody . . . to run the business. Once the court puts
somebody there . . .

PICCOLO: That's it.

PROFACI: This business is one of the worst named businesses in the country because of the criminal element
that's involved . . . with the garbage business, okay?
So all's they gotta have is a little bit of a pinhole and
they gonna, shhhh, rip it right out. You know. That's
what . . .

PICCOLO: Sure . . . exactly what's gonna happen. . . . They don't see that.

PROFACI: They don't give a shit, okay? And you can't, you can't talk. You talk to these people and you know, you say, well, you making a fool of me, shame on you. . . . See, you kill me, it ain't gonna end the problem. . . . You kill Sal, that ain't gonna end the problem . . . because his family, his estate, they gonna take this thing . . . for satisfaction.

PICCOLO: Sure.

PROFACI: But don't they see this? . . . They don't give a damn, John, about nothin' and nobody. You see, so that's the bad situation.

PICCOLO: Then we leave it the way it is now, Sal?

PROFACI: Definitely. We are waiting for Mister Damino to come back to us . . .

PICCOLO: Make a decision.

PROFACI: . . . with some kind of an intelligent decision.

After the saga of the trash dispute, Profaci discussed the "problems" that were pulling his own organization apart. Profaci had been out of prison for about two years after doing time on a conspiracy conviction, and he was quick to tell Piccolo and Stanfa of his dismay over the state of affairs within La Cosa Nostra.

"You know, to me Cosa Nostra's very sacred," Profaci said as the tapes were rolling.

What followed was Profaci's take on the Colombo war that had left a dozen mob members dead in New York and New Jersey. The battle pitted those aligned with imprisoned mob boss Carmine "The Snake" Persico against those loyal to Victor "Little Vic" Orena.

Orena, to whom Profaci swore allegiance, was named acting boss when Persico went to prison in the mid 1980s. But in 1990, from his jail cell, Persico tried to put his son, Junior Persico, in charge. Orena was told to step down, but refused. Attempts to negotiate the problem failed, even when leaders of the other New York families tried to intervene. Instead, both sides resorted to violence.

Turmoil, both Profaci and Piccolo knew, was part of the Brooklyn-based Colombo family legacy. Profaci's father, Joseph, died of natural causes in 1962, but at the time he was at war with a rival faction in his own organization headed by Joseph "Crazy Joey" Gallo. Joe Profaci was succeeded by Joseph Colombo, who gave the family its current name.

Colombo was paralyzed after being shot in 1971 at an Italian American civil rights rally in New York. Gallo, who was suspected of being behind that shooting, was gunned down a year later while eating scampi at Umberto's Clam House, paving the way for Persico's move to the top.

But in 1986, following his conviction in the now famous "Mafia Commission trial," Persico was sentenced to 100 years in jail. For a time, he tried to run the family from prison. Then, in 1989, he appointed Orena acting boss.

Things went along smoothly for the first two years of this arrangement, but in 1991 they deteriorated. The violence and lack of order upset Profaci. So did the elder Persico's attempt to use the media to keep his name current. The jailed mob boss had apparently floated the idea of giving interviews to several national television news magazines, including *60 Minutes* and Barbara Walters's *20/20*. Profaci couldn't understand it. Nor could he hide his outrage over an apparent attempt by Carmine Sessa, the family consiglière who later became a government witness, to set Orena up for a hit. Sessa had been ordered by Orena to poll the leadership of the 125-member Colombo family to determine who wanted Junior Persico to take over and who favored Orena.

For weeks, Sessa ignored the order, Profaci said. Then, instead of an answer, Orena spotted a hit team waiting in a car outside his house.

After that, Profaci said, the shooting started. In all, a dozen members of the organization had been killed and a dozen more had survived murder attempts. The leaders of the other New York families had tried to intervene, to work out a cease fire, but they had failed.

It was, Profaci said, a sad and disgraceful situation. He and Piccolo agreed there was a time and a place for murder, but this was not it.

"If a guy's a rat, sure, then it's honorable."

PROFACI: See, this trouble, this trouble we got?

PICCOLO: We created it.

PROFACI: My representative today is Victor Orena. Victor Orena is a gentleman. Beautiful person. Very, very capable. Very, very qualified. Levelheaded. This guy [Persico] . . .

PICCOLO: Crazy. . . . Put the screws right to you.

PROFACI: Listen to this, June fifteenth, we are sitting together. Victor comes in and his face is, he says, "Sal, boys," he says, "I can't take no more of this."

PICCOLO: It's that bad?

PROFACI: What's the matter? He says, "The guy keeps nailin' me, nailin' me, nailin' me. Because Carmine Persico is losing his mind. Carmine Persico is calling press conferences. Carmine Persico this. Carmine Persico that. Carmine Persico here. He wants to go on *60 Minutes, 20/20.* Walter. Barbara Walters interview here. Interview there. And he keeps telling me that we are nothing. That nobody recognizes us . . . because this guy is doing all these dirty things and we are tell-

ing you to straighten out your family problems. Blah,
blah, blah, blah, blah, blah." He calls his consiglière,
the consiglière is a young guy, I don't know where the
hell he come from. But he's there, Carmine Sessa,
young guy, and he tells, "Carmine," he says, "you
must talk to all our *capodecina*. Talk to the men. Explain to them the pressures that they're putting on us
because of this Persico carrying on. Then let's get an
understanding. Let's see how we all feel about this."

PICCOLO: Sure. Sure.

PROFACI: It went in one ear and out the other. . . . Two
weeks later, we still got no answer. "Carmine, did you
poll the people, did you get a feeling?" "Well, no, I
didn't have . . ." "Whatta you mean, two weeks. This
is serious." He says, "I want it done now. Before tonight, you make it your business to reach everybody."
The following day, four or five guys were sitting in the
car at Victor's house.

STANFA: Yeah. He mentioned it to me!

PROFACI: Okay . . . alright. Because we are a hundred
and twenty, a hundred and twenty-five people. Twenty
people want to stay where they were. A hundred people say, no, we don't agree with what he's [Persico]
doing and he's got a hundred-year sentence, therefore
we can't stay without a family. We can't say that today you in charge, tomorrow I'm in charge. I mean,
that's no way to live. You gotta have a family. You
gotta have a, a share. And that was the beginning of
the trouble. Okay? Now these guys, they say, you
know, nobody told us nothin'. Junior's the boss. Believe in Junior. Because it's Junior's brother to Junior's nephew, about five cousins. You know? It's one,
one big family that they got. In the meantime, that's
now. Now we started shooting and where's it gonna
end? . . . It's sick because, why John? That's no reason.

STANFA: Ah, like a Tony said, I agree with Tony . . . because we no do this.

PROFACI: Yeah, the bastard. . . . In the meantime, this

guy [Persico] says that this guy's nobody. This guy is nobody. This guy is nobody. . . . Over here, nobody's nobody. . . . I say, "What are you talking about." I mean, I knew these people all my life. What are you gonna tell me that I can't respect these people. For what?

PICCOLO: Crazy.

PROFACI: He's the only one. He's the only one that's any good.

PICCOLO: In the family it's like a chain. You keep breaking the beads, forget about it.

PROFACI: So, it's, uh, you know, I feel very bad. Because, really, we're all basically good people.

PICCOLO: Damn right.

PROFACI: And it's no honor when we kill one another.

PICCOLO: Nah.

STANFA: Now . . .

PROFACI: No. It's no honor.

STANFA: . . . . they give, see, they give satisfaction.

PROFACI: I mean, if this guy . . . I mean, if a guy's a rat or if a guy . . .

STANFA: 'Cause he deserve it. Yes.

PROFACI: Jesus Christ. In a minute. But why . . .

PICCOLO: Of course. That's honorable.

STANFA: We not too much over here. We don't have too much of a problem. Everything like that.

PICCOLO: Believe me, when I say this, and I'm not trying to patronize you in any way. . . . I was raised . . . right. In This Thing . . . my father was originally in Brooklyn. Now I'm going back into the twenties. . . . Your family, more than any other family, was always honorable. Not that you're sitting here.

PROFACI: Listen. I know my father. I knew the man he was. My father died with a broken heart . . . because he couldn't, he says, "I can't believe that these people gonna turn against me. Why? . . . I can't believe it." But there was The Snake.

PICCOLO: The Snake.

STANFA: That's all I say. This is another thing, you know

to me, we have a problem. We can't find no more people qualified for this . . .

PICCOLO: But John, John let me say this to you . . .

STANFA: And between us, believe me, see people . . .
they started thinking what they're supposed to be. Not
like a friend. It is supposed to be like a brother.

PICCOLO: . . . if we're five, then we're five good ones.

PROFACI: Yeah.

PICCOLO: Worth a hundred bad ones.

The same problems Profaci described within his own
crime family would come to haunt Stanfa and Piccolo.
The clash of personalities and the divided loyalties that
were undermining the Colombo organization in New
York soon would dominate the Philadelphia underworld
as well.

The first shots in a mob war that would wreck the
Stanfa organization were fired six weeks later on a quiet
streetcorner in the heart of South Philadelphia. Although
few people in law enforcement or mob circles realized
it at the time, that's when Stanfa began to lose control
of the organization he was supposed to be putting back
together.

But in December 1992, it was just the tapes, not the
potential mob war, that attracted law enforcement attention.

"Grand slam," said the FBI agents from their listening post as Profaci and Piccolo talked openly about La
Cosa Nostra. "Grand slam."

5

Felix Bocchino was a survivor, an underworld realist.

He had spent more than fifty years making a comfortable living as a mob-connected bookmaker, extortionist, and drug trafficker, negotiating the murky underworld where ever-shifting alliances and petty backstabbing often proved fatal.

In January of 1992, at the age of seventy-three, he was still active and, according to law enforcement sources, was emerging as a player in the Stanfa organization. He was running a bookmaking operation in South Philadelphia and had begun to collect a street tax from gamblers in Northeast Philadelphia, one of the first moves by the Stanfa crime family to reestablish its control of the underworld gambling market.

In the 1980s, Little Nicky Scarfo had generated hundreds of thousands of dollars from the street tax, an extortion racket that required gamblers, loan sharks, and drug dealers not directly aligned with the mob to pay a weekly or monthly stipend to the organization in order to stay in business.

It was a simple proposition: Pay or die.

After Scarfo and his top associates were convicted and sent to prison, the street tax disappeared. Independent

bookmakers and loan sharks had been on their own, doing business without any underworld interference, for
about five years. Now that was changing. While Stanfa
paid lip service to the traditions of honor and loyalty
that were the cornerstones of the Mafia, he was in many
ways as greedy and arrogant as Scarfo. The street tax
was one example. It was a quick, easy way to generate
cash. That it created an atmosphere filled with tension
and threats of violence and attracted law enforcement
were secondary concerns. When money was involved,
Stanfa, like Scarfo, was single-minded.

Felix Bocchino got up every morning around 7 A.M.
to take his dog for a walk and buy the morning paper.
Then he'd return to the second-floor apartment on East
Passyunk Avenue that he shared with his daughter.
There he'd leave the dog, get in his car, and drive to a
local diner for breakfast. That was the routine he followed on the morning of January 29. He had just slid
behind the wheel of his two-door, maroon Buick when
a man wearing a hooded black jacket ran up to the car
and opened fire.

The gunman pumped four shots through the driver's
side window. Two bullets from the .38-caliber handgun
ripped through Bocchino's neck. Another crashed into
his temple. A fourth grazed the bridge of his nose before
shattering the passenger-side window of the car.

Bocchino died sitting behind the steering wheel, his
car keys in the ignition, his morning paper on the seat
beside him. Police found $1,000 in cash in his wallet.

The murder was portrayed in the media as the first
mob hit in seven years. Television anchormen and newspaper reporters speculated ominously about the start of

a new mob war, but police were more circumspect. Among the early reports was law enforcement speculation that Stanfa might have been behind the killing. Questioned by detectives, Stanfa was described as nervous and uncooperative. He then dropped out of sight.

Federal authorities, however, had their own theory about what was going on in the underworld. Aided by snippets of conversation picked up in Avena's law office in January and February—not every conversation was clear and to the point, nor was every conversation picked up in its entirety—the feds knew that Stanfa had a problem with a group of young mobsters who were balking at his attempts to take over the organization. These were the sons, brothers, and nephews of Scarfo crime family members. They had been born and raised in South Philadelphia and embraced the street corner mentality that is both a boon and a bane in the neighborhood.

Stanfa's Sicilian pedigree, while a plus among the older generation of mobsters in New York and Philadelphia, meant nothing to the young kids on the corner. This was their city. He was an outsider who had no standing.

Eventually the group of young mob wannabes would be identified in the media as the "Young Turks," a designation that a federal judge would later naively question, pointing out that none of them were of Turkish descent. The niceties—or inanities—of political correctness aside, the Bocchino hit is now considered the first shooting in the battle between Stanfa and a group of young mob rivals that would last two years.

In the weeks that followed the Bocchino murder, investigators developed a second possible—and probably accurate—motive for the shooting. Several of the bookmakers in Northeast Philadelphia who Bocchino approached for a street tax were already paying. But they were paying the young South Philadelphia mobsters. Bocchino was putting his hand in their pockets. The fact that Stanfa was backing Bocchino meant nothing. To the young mobsters, Stanfa was still a "greaser," a "greaseball," a "Siggie," someone who couldn't find his way up Broad Street on New Year's Day, someone who didn't know or understand Philadelphia—someone who didn't belong.

On February 24, 1992, agents monitoring the bugs in Avena's office picked up part of a conversation between Piccolo and Avena in which the Bocchino shooting was discussed. Piccolo, according to an FBI report later filed under court seal, said he knew who was responsible for the murder and that plans for a retaliatory strike were in place. Piccolo said he, himself, was not involved in those plans. He and Avena also discussed "letting those responsible into the Family in order to make retaliation easier," a scheme that Stanfa later adopted.

On Tuesday evening, March 3, Michael Ciancaglini, a strapping, twenty-nine-year-old mobster, was walking back to his rowhouse on McKean Street after a game of basketball in the neighborhood. Ciancaglini's father, Joseph "Chick" Ciancaglini, a capo in the Scarfo organization, was serving forty-five years in federal prison after being convicted with Scarfo and fourteen others in a 1988 RICO case. An older brother, John, was doing a seven-year stint for extortion.

A second brother, Joseph "Joe Chang" Ciancaglini Jr., was aligned with Stanfa. Michael, however, was considered part of the Young Turk faction. Despite an underworld philosophy built around family and bloodlines, the Philadelphia mob had a long history of father fighting against son and brother against brother. The Ciancaglinis were about to become a part of that inexplicable phenomenon.

Mike Ciancaglini walked past a Ford station wagon parked on the corner of his block. As he did so, two men armed with shotguns jumped out of the vehicle. Ciancaglini began to run for his life, sprinting for his front door with the gunmen in pursuit. He reached his house in the middle of the block, rushed through the door and slammed it behind him. The gunmen fired two rounds through the door and two more through the living room window where Ciancaglini's wife, Monique, was sitting. Their two children, aged two and three, were upstairs at the time.

Neither Ciancaglini nor his wife were hit. The gunmen continued to run down the block and disappeared, along with the station wagon. Police recovered more than twenty shotgun pellets from the ceiling and archway between the living room and dining room of the home. The wrought-iron and glass-enclosed front door and front window were destroyed. Outside, investigators found five 12-gauge shotgun shells.

Ciancaglini, questioned by detectives, provided few details.

"He don't know why, he don't know who, and he don't know what," said Joe Santaguida, his lawyer.

Police immediately theorized, however, that the shooting was in response to the Bocchino killing. And now they, too, warned about a potential mob war.

"There appears to be a faction . . . who don't want to fall in line under Stanfa," said one investigator.

"There's a certain amount of parochialism," added another veteran mob watcher who put his finger on the heart of the problem. "And there's also a generational thing. In the short term, these kids could cause some problems. But in the long term, Stanfa has the clout and the support. . . . There could be more bloodshed before it's over."

Police said Michael Ciancaglini was the number two man in a fledgling organization headed by Joseph "Skinny Joey" Merlino, the handsome and charismatic son of former Scarfo underboss Salvatore Merlino. Others linked to Merlino and Mike Ciancaglini by federal authorities included Steven Mazzone, Marty Angelina, George Borgesi—whose uncle was an imprisoned Scarfo hit man—Gaetano "Tommy Horsehead" Scafidi, whose brother was another imprisoned Scarfo shooter, and Vince Iannece, whose father was a jailed Scarfo soldier.

While much would be made over the next two years about how the young gangsters had formed a "faction" in opposition to Stanfa, the simple fact of the matter was that most of them had grown up together, gone to the same Catholic grammar school, attended the same high school, and hung for all of their lives on the same corner. They might have been the "Young Turks" to the media and, eventually, the "Merlino mob faction" to the feds, but before all of that, they were the guys from Twelfth and Wolf and the Epiphany parish. And, ironically, those roots would prove to be deeper and stronger than the Mafia blood oath and the code of *omertà* around which Stanfa tried to build his organization.

At the time Mike Ciancaglini was ambushed, Joey Merlino was in federal prison, finishing up a sentence for an armored truck heist in which over $350,000 had been taken. Merlino, convicted when two of his accomplices cooperated and testified for the government, served more than two years of a four-year sentence before earning parole. The money was never recovered. A federal prosecutor said the jail time didn't bother the young mobster—Merlino considered it the cost of doing business.

The business—more than a quarter of a million tax free dollars—was very profitable.

On March 6, three days after the botched Mike Ciancaglini hit, FBI agents watching Avena's office recorded the separate arrivals of Piccolo, Stanfa, and Joe Ciancaglini but their listening devices picked up very little. There was, according to one report, a brief, whispered conversation involving Stanfa, Ciancaglini and Avena. Stanfa and Ciancaglini left the office together that afternoon at 3:26 P.M.

A week later, on March 13, there was another short conversation in which Piccolo told Avena that Stanfa was "not staying still anywhere," one of the first indications federal authorities had that the mob boss believed he might be targeted. Three days later, Piccolo told Avena the rumor on the street was that the young renegades were looking to hit Joey Ciancaglini. During that conversation, FBI agents later reported, Avena asked if the hit on Michael Ciancaglini was supposed to go off the way it did. In other words, was the shooting a warning rather than a botched murder. Piccolo indicated that it wasn't planned as a miss.

"Well, what a sloppy job," said Avena.

"You've answered the question," replied Piccolo.

"That was the worst thing that could have happened."

On March 17, Stanfa visited Avena and told him that he believed Michael Ciancaglini and members of the "Young Turks" were looking for him. As a precaution, Stanfa said he would need a day's notice if Avena wanted to see him. The two then arranged a coded telephone call system that Avena could use to reach the mob boss. While law enforcement authorities believed that Stanfa, with the backing of the Gambino organization out of New York and his Mafia cousins in Palermo, had the upper hand in a battle against a handful of South Philadelphia corner boys, the conversations picked up in Avena's office painted a picture of a less confident, even paranoid, Mafia boss.

The fact that they didn't have a clearer picture of the situation at the time was one of the frustrations of the investigation. A series of FBI reports—the ten-day accounts submitted with each request for an extension of the eavesdropping—detailed some of the surveillance problems.

The listening devices could only be turned on when mobsters had been spotted entering the office. Even then, agents manning the monitors had to run a spot-check to determine if a conversation was relevant to the investigation. Conversations that Piccolo had with Avena concerning pending legal matters, for example, could not be monitored or recorded. At the time, Avena was representing Piccolo in a state racketeering case scheduled for trial in New Jersey Superior Court in Camden. If the feds shut down their wires because the topic was a legal one, they'd have to spot-check from time to time to see if the topic had changed. As a result, some conversations would be missed, or picked up in midstream. These could often be confusing because of the lack of context.

At other times, the feds and the unwitting mobsters played a game of electronic cat-and-mouse. The agents would spot-check the conference room and Avena's office on a regular basis when they knew Stanfa, Piccolo, or any other significant wiseguy was in the building. But if, as the agents later learned, the mobsters were meeting in another room—frequently they would use the private office of any one of the other lawyers who weren't in that day—there was no way for the conversations to be recorded.

So while some of the FBI reports were loaded with valuable intelligence, others were cluttered with the minutiae of surveillance work:

"Two spot-checks in the office revealed no pertinent conversations."

"One spot-check in each area revealed only background noise."

"Spot-checks in the office and monitoring in the conference room revealed no pertinent conversations."

"A spot-check in Avena's office revealed the end of a conversation between Joseph Profaci and Salvatore Avena regarding the looting of the garbage business."

"Spot-checks in the office and conference room revealed no conversation until 2:23 P.M. when a conversation was intercepted in Avena's office involving Avena, Stanfa, and Piccolo. Some of the conversation was conducted in whispers. In a portion of the conversation which was discernable, Stanfa arranged a code with Avena to confirm a scheduled meeting."

Still more frustrating was when someone the feds had a real interest in entered the office, but could not be located electronically. On April 8, for example, FBI

agents surveilling 519 Market Street noted the arrival at
1:24 P.M. of Giuseppe Gambino.

Giuseppe, Rosario, and Giovanni Gambino were dis-
tant Sicilian cousins of the late Carlo Gambino. They
had set up shop in South Jersey in the 1970s with the
approval of Angelo Bruno and had established, through
restaurants and pizza shops, a heroin distribution network that was part of the infamous Pizza Connection,
the international Mafia heroin ring.

Rosario was serving a federal sentence for drug trafficking in 1992. Giuseppe was in New York with his
brother, Giovanni (or John). John Gambino, according
to federal authorities, was, like Stanfa, a hybrid Mafioso.
He was part of a Sicilian mob clan but was also a capo
in the Gambino family headed by John Gotti. Both John
and Giuseppe Gambino would eventually be convicted
in New York of drug trafficking. In fact, Sammy the
Bull Gravano would testify against them.

At the time that Giuseppe Gambino visited Avena's
office, both he and his brother were targets of a federal
drug probe, all the more reason why agents wanted to
hear what he had to say to Piccolo and Stanfa, who had
entered the office about an hour before he arrived. Donald Manno, a lawyer who sometimes represented Piccolo, was there as well.

From the FBI surveillance report of April 8, 1992:

At 1:24 P.M. Giuseppe Gambino entered 519 Market
Street. Monitoring in Avena's office revealed that
Manno, Avena, and others were having lunch there. Piccolo and Stanfa were not in Avena's office. Monitoring
in the conference room failed to locate Piccolo or

Stanfa. Stanfa departed at 1:46 P.M., Gambino departed
at 1:59 P.M., and Piccolo departed with Manno.

Stanfa's Sicilian connections had always intrigued authorities, so much so that one of the agents assigned to
coordinate the investigation was Paul A. Hayes Jr.
Hayes, a veteran investigator and aficionado of all things
Italian, had been a member of the Philadelphia office's
Sicilian squad before being transferred to the traditional
LCN squad that was targeting Stanfa. He dressed in designer suits and highly polished leather loafers. His
sandy-gray hair was coiffed rather than cut, and hung
down over the starched white collars of his expensive
dress shirts. He spoke Italian, read an Italian newspaper
on a regular basis, and subscribed to an Italian magazine.
He was equally at home discussing Roman politics or
pasta, and brought a sophistication to the investigation
that belied his gumshoe nature.

Hayes and Steve Salvo—an FBI linguistic expert who
was born in Sicily, spoke Sicilian, and was used to trans-
late many of the Stanfa tapes—had been tracking the
local Sicilian connection for several years and were fas-
cinated by the occasional overlaps with the Stanfa organization. Like the trash hauling business and the
Colombo war, it is an area still being investigated.

Both Salvo and Hayes grudgingly admit the Sicilians
will be harder to crack than the Stanfa organization that,
for all of Stanfa's bravado and posturing, operated in a
slipshod manner that made it possible for the feds to
quickly build a case.

In contrast, Salvo and Hayes described how they were
once assigned to watch a suspected member of a Sicilian
drug network who was living just outside of Philadelphia

where he operated a pizza shop. One day, Salvo said, they tailed the suspect on a forty-five-mile car ride to a pay phone at a highway rest stop. There the suspect got out of his car and waited several minutes until the phone rang. He then spoke for less than a minute, Salvo said, before hanging up, getting back in his car and driving home.

"Forty-five miles each way for a thirty-second phone call," said Salvo. "These guys are serious about what they do."

For years, members of the Sicilian mob had operated separately from the American Cosa Nostra in and around Philadelphia and South Jersey. Authorities believed Angelo Bruno had reached an accomodation with them and willingly accepted a stipend that came from the drug profits the Sicilians generated in his area. At the same time, Bruno refused to allow members of his own organization to traffic in narcotics. This hypocrisy rankled many of the mob boss's top associates, particularly his consiglière, Tony Bananas Caponigro, who saw the profits that could be made dealing drugs. It may have been one of the reasons Bruno was killed.

Scarfo, who followed Bruno, disdained the Sicilians— in part because his ancestry was Calabrian, and in part because he feared them.

Stanfa, on the other hand, was a *paisano*. Had Stanfa managed to stay in power, many believe the Sicilian mob would have eventually exerted full and total control over the Philadelphia–South Jersey area.

Evidence of the Sicilian mob's influence over Stanfa surfaced during the FBI investigation in 1992. Little of it came out during the trial, however. Stanfa and Joe Ciancaglini, for example, were tailed to Long Island on at least two occasions to meet with a suspected Sicilian heroin kingpin and, for a time at least, local police worked on a theory that Stanfa's imported food distribution company might have been a front for drug trafficking. Nothing ever came of that investigation, however.

Even more tantalizing was a report in *The New York Times* in June 1992 about the brutal assassination one month earlier of celebrated anti-Mafia prosecutor Giovanni Falcone. Falcone, his wife, and their bodyguards were blown up on a highway outside of Palermo when their car drove over a Mafia-planted bomb. At the time of his death, *The Times* reported, Falcone had undertaken two new investigations. One focused on a Sicilian drug link with a Colombian cocaine cartel. The other "was the recruitment of Mafia soldiers in Sicily and their transfer to Cosa Nostra in Philadelphia," Italian Justice Minister Claudio Martelli told *The Times*.

Federal authorities knew that two young Sicilians living in Philadelphia, Biagio Adornetto and Rosario Bellocchi, were active in Stanfa's organization. Stanfa led them to believe that they would eventually have special standing because of their ancestry. There would come a time, Adornetto was told, when Stanfa would get rid of all the Americans. Americans weren't suited for life in the Mafia, Stanfa said. They didn't understand La Cosa Nostra. Stanfa also fawned over Sergio Battaglia, another young recruit who had come to the United States with his family from southern Italy about fifteen years earlier. Battaglia, like Adornetto and Bellocchi, was in his twenties, but his lack of experience wasn't as important as his Italian bloodlines.

On May 5, 1992, a federal court judge in Camden

authorized a second expansion of the eavesdropping at
519 Market Street. Another surreptitious entry was approved and now bugs were in place at nine different
locations, including the offices of other lawyers, the library, the television room, and the lunch room.

Also in that first week in May, "Skinny Joey" Merlino returned to South Philadelphia. Paroled after serving
more than two years for the armored truck heist, Merlino
took his place beside Mike Ciancaglini as a leader of
the young American faction of the Philadelphia mob.

Dealing with Merlino and Mike Ciancaglini became
a major concern for Stanfa that spring and summer. Federal authorities watched with fascination as the mob boss
began to maneuver them into a position for a kill. Stanfa
subscribed to the same philosophy as several veteran
Philadelphia organized crime figures who had become
informants. In order to stay alive and on top in the underworld, they said, "You gotta keep your friends close
and your enemies closer."

Friends, enemies, life, and death were themes that
cropped up repeatedly in another series of conversations
in Avena's office about the ongoing and still unresolved
trash dispute.

In January, despite the concerns expressed by Profaci,
Avena had lawyers file a civil racketeering suit in US
District Court in Philadelphia alleging that Carmine
Franco had depleted the assets of their two companies,
AAA Waste Disposal Corp. and Philadelphia Recyling
and Transfer Station Inc., through a pattern of fraud,
misrepresentation, and breach of contract. The language
was standard for a civil RICO suit. So was the demand
for triple damages, which would have amounted to mil-

lions of dollars. But along with the legal papers, the lawyers for Avena had filed part of a 1990 Pennsylvania Crime Commission Report that described Franco's alleged mob connections.

Neither Profaci nor the mob leaders he answered to in New York were pleased.

6

**FBI Surveillance Tape
June 2, 1992
2:49 P.M.**

SALVATORE AVENA: Did I do somethin' wrong?
SALVATORE PROFACI: Well, we started a lawsuit. Goodfellows don't sue goodfellows. . . . Goodfellows kill
  goodfellows.

Of all the quotes on all the tapes from all the conversations made during the FBI's four-year investigation of
the Philadelphia mob, none compare to Sal Profaci's
succinct and chilling explanation that spring afternoon.

It was the essence of wiseguy life and it quickly became the signature phrase of the ongoing probe.

Francis Ford Coppola and Mario Puzo rode to fame
and fortune on a similar line—"I'll make him an offer
he can't refuse"—but that was make believe. This was
real life. Or maybe it was life imitating art. Sometimes
the agents in the courthouse basement couldn't be sure.
Sometimes the dialogue and the setting were just too
good. Sometimes, it seemed as if it had all been scripted
by Coppola or Scorsese or, when things really got crazy,
Tarantino.

Sal Avena's law offices occupied the entire second floor of a nondescript two-story building in downtown Camden, New Jersey, just across the Ben Franklin Bridge from center city Philadelphia. City Hall and the Camden County Probation Department were right across the street. The County Hall of Justice was around the corner. The US Post Office and federal courthouse were a block away.

Avena, an avuncular man noted for his polite and courtly manner, had operated out of that address for decades, representing a coterie of criminal defendants including the late Angelo Bruno, Stanfa, Piccolo, and several reputed South Jersey mob figures. In his late sixties and at the end of what had been a prosperous and professionally successful law career, Avena was regarded as a competent, well-connected attorney. He had a gorgeous home in one of the suburban communities outside of Camden and another on the beach at the Jersey shore near Sea Isle City.

Unlike other high profile mob attorneys—Bruce Cutler in New York or Bobby Simone in Philadelphia for example—Avena was not a flamboyant or aggressive courtroom advocate. But more often than not, he got the job done in his studied and, some might say, plodding manner. His standing with many of his more notorious clients was enhanced because of his family background. His father, John Avena, had been a Philadelphia Mafia boss in the early 1930s. He was murdered gangland-style when Sal Avena was just ten years old.

Avena and his widowed mother moved to New Jersey, where he grew up in the home of an aunt and uncle. He worked his way through college and law school with menial jobs in the factories and warehouses that were a part of the industrial boom along the Delaware River in both New Jersey and Pennsylvania at the time.

Nevertheless, it is part of the folklore of the mob that Avena and his mother were looked after by organized crime figures after his father's death and that Avena's education, including his law school studies, was paid for by the organization. That apparent fiction added to the mystique that surrounded Avena where the wiseguys were concerned.

"I mean this fella comes from an honorable family," Anthony Piccolo said in one conversation in which he was defending Avena in the trash dispute with Franco. "And here's his father that gave his life for this family. Jesus Christ, don't we respect each other anymore?

"I mean, Christ almighty, he does favors. . . . He don't take advantage of anybody. He breaks his neck for everybody and this is the way he's gonna be treated?"

Avena's alleged mob ties became a secondary, but nonetheless fascinating, part of the Stanfa investigation. His eventual indictment in 1994 along with Stanfa and some twenty other mob members or associates shocked many of those who knew him as one of the elder statesmen of the South Jersey criminal defense bar. His subsequent acquittal two years later provided him with a public exoneration that took some, but not all, of the sting out of the public perception generated by the investigation and the publication of most of the taped conversations picked up in his office.

Clearly, Avena was sucked into the quagmire of the Stanfa investigation because of the dispute with Franco over the trash business. Through it all he insisted he did nothing wrong, nothing illegal, nothing improper. As a lawyer, he said, he was offering legitimate counsel to

Stanfa, Piccolo, and the others when he met with them. What they said outside of his presence he could not control, nor should he be held accountable for those discussions. And as a businessman who felt he was being cheated, his move to sue Franco in a court of law was both justifiable and the proper course of action—hardly, he further argued, the course a mobster would take to settle a dispute.

Few people who knew Camden were surprised when they learned how easily and how often the FBI broke into 519 Market Street.

"It wasn't exactly real secure," said a lawyer who once worked in the building. "There would be mornings when we'd arrive at work and the alarm would be ringing, but the police hadn't shown up. We used to put a two-by-four against the back door. It wasn't a real sophisticated alarm system."

The bugging was carried out under cover of darkness and, to this day, the FBI has said little about the "black bag" operation. But breaking into the office was probably a piece of cake for the government's second-story men. None of the stores or businesses on the block are open after dark. Neither are any of the city, county, or federal buildings. Pedestrian traffic dries up once the office workers have gone home at 5 P.M. By midnight the streets are literally deserted. Agents trained at jimmying locks and thwarting alarm systems would have had little in the way of outside distraction as they went about their business. They got in and got out, locking the doors behind them. After that it was simply a matter of waiting, watching, and listening.

There was one bit of irony, however.

Hanging on the wood-paneled wall in Avena's office
was a two-by-three-foot framed poster, a reproduction
from the old World War II "Loose Lips Sink Ships"
campaign. Done in stark blues, blacks, and grays, it was
an eerie picture of a sailor struggling in a dark and
choppy sea. The sailor's face is a grimace as he waves
one arm in the air and frantically struggles to stay atop
the waves cascading around him. In the background is
his sinking ship, half submerged and outlined against the
darkened sky. Superimposed across the troubling scene,
in bold white letters, is the warning, SOMEBODY TALKED.

Stanfa liked the poster so much that he had Avena
make him a copy and later hung it in his own office at
Continental Imported Food Distributors Inc., a South
Philadelphia imported food distribution warehouse run
by his son. He and the other mobsters who met in Avena's office saw it as a reference to informants who, they
all knew, could bring down an organization.

But at 519 Market Street, it was the mobsters themselves who did the talking.

While he was described as a key figure in the Stanfa
criminal enterprise, Sal Avena's dispute with Carmine
Franco and the information gathered by the FBI about
the trash business may ultimately prove to be more important to federal authorities than the lawyer's alleged
role in the Philadelphia mob. Like Avena, Franco has
consistently denied any wrongdoing and has scoffed at
the charges that he is associated with the mob.

"My client . . . never was nor is he presently a member of any organized crime family," Franco's criminal
defense attorney said after the allegations on the Avena
tapes surfaced. "He is a hardworking individual who

through sheer individual effort has achieved a degree of success in the solid waste business. . . . It's an American success story, not an organized crime story.''

Sal Profaci told a different tale.

The New York mobster and his son Joe, Avena's son-in-law, spoke at length about the Franco situation during the June 2 ''goodfellas'' conversation. The Profacis had apparently met with leaders of the Genovese family earlier and were told in no uncertain terms that the lawsuit had to stop. Otherwise, there would be problems.

SALVATORE PROFACI: Sal, I'm really, ya know, I really don't know how to tell you this. I keep tryin', tryin' to make the point, but, ah, you keep missin' the point.

AVENA: No. I just don't want . . . blinders on, that's all, Sal.

SAL PROFACI: I keep tryin' to make you understand that we cannot go any further with this lawsuit. . . . You're gonna forget about it because . . .

AVENA: No way.

SAL PROFACI: . . . you got my life at stake.

AVENA: Yeah? What am I supposed to do?

SAL PROFACI: You're gonna drop the case.

AVENA: I'm gonna drop the case. . . . Blow the money.

SAL PROFACI: Right. . . . Whatever, whatever the money is, money can be earned.

(Later)

AVENA: What do you want me to be, some dunce?

SAL PROFACI: I don't wanna hear it. . . . I don't wanna hear it.

AVENA: You want me to be some dunce . . . sittin' on the side of the desk.

SAL PROFACI: I am just tryin' to guide us through this thing in one piece, okay?

AVENA: I don't know what that means.

SAL PROFACI: Because it's . . . if you're no longer around, or I'm no longer around, we're gonna suffer tremendous. Our family suffers tremendously. . . . Whatever your financial damages will be, we will look to see how it's got to be compensated for.

AVENA: That don't make sense. It tells me nothin'. We will look to see. We've been lookin' for two and a half years. . . . We've been lookin' at ourselves in the mirror like big monkeys.

SAL PROFACI: We have no choice. We have no choice.

AVENA: What you're tellin' me is surrender, give up . . .

SAL PROFACI: That's right.

AVENA: . . . and lose. . . . All of a sudden, my position means nothin' to you.

SAL PROFACI: I got abused today . . .

AVENA: How come we're givin' this . . . presentin' this truffle to Mister Carmine?

SAL PROFACI: I got, I got abused today.

AVENA: Ya know, I know who the whore is.

SAL PROFACI: I got . . . I'm the whore.

AVENA: No.

SAL PROFACI: Me.

AVENA: I know who the whore is.

SAL PROFACI: I'm the whore, okay? I'm the whore because I don't see the whole picture. All right? I got abused . . .

AVENA: I don't believe . . .

SAL PROFACI: . . . today. And I will get plenty of abusement on Tuesday. See? Because today I got abused that I should know better. Then . . .

AVENA: Then do what?

SAL PROFACI: . . . take a goodfella to court.

AVENA: Take a goodfella to court?

SAL PROFACI: Right. Right. That's . . . evidently that's the new rules of the game.

AVENA: Well, I'm not gonna play those rules, Sal.

SAL PROFACI: Well.

AVENA: You started off, Sal. We . . .

SAL PROFACI: I don't wanna hear it.

AVENA: Oh, you don't wanna hear it?

SAL PROFACI: I don't wanna hear it.

AVENA: Well then, what . . .

SAL PROFACI: I don't wanna hear it.

AVENA: . . . what the hell. Nothin' else makes any difference then.

SAL PROFACI: I don't wanna hear it.

AVENA: You might as well go join Carmine, if that's what you're tellin' me. . . . Bring him the truffle.

SAL PROFACI: I don't have to join Carmine. . . . I will take care of Carmine in my own way. . . . I got abused. I got abused today because people that, that we have, people that we sat with have all been named in this thing. Myself included.

(Later)

SAL PROFACI: They're sayin' that we are the cause of destroying everything that they've created in Philadelphia. And plus, by blowing Carmine out of the water, we are destroying their number one earner in the whole organization. That's what they're sayin'.

AVENA: Better that I get blown out of the water?

SAL PROFACI: See? Well, this is what they're sayin' Sal.

AVENA: Okay. What am I supposed to do? Say . . . I'll be the, I'll be the palace guard for Carmine. Let me be the, ah, take the poison.

SAL PROFACI: Let me tell you somethin', ah, we can only go one step at a time. We can't speculate. . . . I said any . . . wrongdoings here was on the part of Carmine Franco because Carmine Franco orchestrated the entire program. He picked the players. He picked, he picked the actors. He picked everything. And he had free reign for five years to do what he wanted to do with whoever he wanted to do it with. Okay? Now, when you, the puppet, and the most abused person that I ever saw in my life, decided that you had enough, that's when you decided to try to see how you could get some justice. Okay? And we started to talk to these people. Eighteen months we talked to these people.

AVENA: Two and a half years.

SAL PROFACI: Eighteen months, okay? And they kept

bullshitting us and bullshitting us and bullshitting us. Okay? . . . The last bullshit was on November tenth, or November twentieth, to be exact, a week before Thanksgiving, when they promised to deliver the credit to your company in New Jersey.

JOSEPH PROFACI: They never . . . and they've never said that you guys were, ah, or they never actually looked to defend Carmine that he didn't do what we said he did.

AVENA: Well, let him do what's right. Let him put it on the table where . . .

JOE PROFACI: Ah, I think, I'm afraid that the whole thing's gonna blow sky high with, ah, with three initials.

AVENA: I don't know what ya mean, three initials.

JOE PROFACI: The feds [FBI].

(Later)

SAL PROFACI: Ya wanna know the truth, Sal? . . . There hasn't been a one discussion on money. That's basically what ya wanna know.

AVENA: Well, what do they say should be the terms by which this case ends.

SAL PROFACI: Well, let me tell ya somethin' Sal. I, I see, I see a lot of bad things coming because, ya know, ah, from altogether wrong, okay? Which he didn't have a leg to stand on. They usin' this suit as now, he is the victim.

AVENA: Where does it give him a leg to stand on?

SAL PROFACI: Because we're goodfellas.

AVENA: What was going against anybody that's a goodfella.

SAL PROFACI: Well, Carmine's a goodfella.

AVENA: What's that mean? That nobody else is good here, then?

(Later)

SAL PROFACI: Sal, we've got to buy time. Got to buy time. And . . . see what I don't, what I could see . . . ya see Carmine. I don't see where he had any way out of this problem that he had down here. And the lawsuit gave

him an out. See. Because now, with the lawsuit, he
could go to his people and cry that, ya see what they
did to me. I've been bringing you people all this money
and now look what they did to me. So now they're all
comin' out of the closets.

AVENA: Sal, he's shootin' himself in the foot . . .

SAL PROFACI: I'm waitin' to see, okay? So, again, like I
say, I wanna see who the players are, cause I don't
see who the players are. They know who we are, I
don't know who they are. I know Carmine Franco.
See? And I don't know if, I'm not sure, if eliminating
Carmine Franco solves every problem. But when I
know who the players are, that's a different story.

(Later)

AVENA: Sal, what do ya make of it. The whole situation.

SAL PROFACI: It stinks. It stinks.

AVENA: Without anybody in this room. Tell me, what one
thing have I done wrong here?

SAL PROFACI: We started a lawsuit and they're capitali-
zin' on the fact that he's a goodfellow and we started
a lawsuit.

AVENA: Did I do somethin' wrong?

SAL PROFACI: Well, we started a lawsuit. Goodfellows
don't sue goodfellows.

AVENA: Goodfellows don't sue goodfellows? So the thief
could do as he pleases and that's it?

SAL PROFACI: Goodfellows kill goodfellows. I guess that's
where it's at.

A week later, after apparently meeting again in New
York to discuss the dispute, Sal Profaci returned to Av-
ena's office, this time with an offer to settle the suit.
Piccolo was also present for the discussion.

"They're gonna take you out of all responsibilities
and you're gonna receive a payment of two [million dol-
lars] for your share," Profaci told Avena. "Sal, please
. . . Carmine Franco is no longer in your life. Hopefully.
Okay? Hopefully."

"That's right," Piccolo added. "Now, what do ya
say, ya make the best of a bad situation?'

But it was not to be.

The "bad situation" would linger for the rest of 1992
and, as with almost everything else involving the Stanfa
crime family at this time, the feds would get most of it
on tape. Carmine Franco was not out of Avena's life.
The trash dispute continued. Franco apparently wasn't
any more willing than Avena to accept an imposed settlement. He filed a counterclaim in federal court alleging
that it was Avena, with mob backing, who was trying
to force him out of the business. That move escalated
the stakes in the lawsuit and, potentially, could have
shed even more light on organized crime's involvement
in the trash business. Profaci, caught in the middle, felt
the pressure building. He, more than Avena or Franco,
realized what was at stake. He was being held responsible for settling the issue, but he knew that the final
negotiating tool might not be a lawyer's pen or a judge's
gavel.

In one heated argument with Avena that summer, he
said, "I'm trying to keep us alive, that's what I'm trying
to do." In another, after Avena once again went into
detail about the legal issues and his conviction that he
would win a lawsuit, Profaci blurted out, "You're playing with my life and my kid's life, that's exactly what
you're doing." Even if Avena were to win a huge mon-
etary settlement, Profaci added, "You and your children,
me and my children will not live to enjoy it."

Profaci's continued attempts to settle the issue in "the
court of honor" rather than "the court of law" generated more valuable and incriminating evidence for "the
three initials" and led to a series of additional meetings

in Avena's office, including a December 16 sitdown that brought Profaci, Big Billy D'Elia—an alleged leader of the Bufalino organization in upstate Pennsylvania—and Stanfa and Piccolo together with Avena.

It was another unprecedented development in an investigation that just seemed to get better and better. Here were the leaders of three different mob families sitting down to discuss mob business. Once again the FBI got it all—the tough talk, the angry recriminations, and the classic gangland repartee of well-connected wiseguys clearly at ease and without a clue anyone was listening.

"See, Sal, the difference is, he is a street guy. You're not a street guy.... They're two different breeds. In other words, when this guy is making moves and you're doing it straight, you don't have a shot."

D'Elia was holding court in the conference room for Avena, Profaci, Stanfa, and Piccolo. The burly, six-foot-four, 240-pound mobster said he had been asked by Franco and the Genovese family to help Profaci settle the dispute. Once again, the two-million dollar offer was on the table. Once again, Avena was told to take the deal. This time, he was assured, Franco would go along. He, too, had gotten the word.

There had been other options, D'Elia joked, but they were no longer available.

"The answer was that when he [Franco] was standing by the [trash] trucks, somebody should have bumped him in and let them compact him."

Of course this might have caused some problems with the Genovese organization, Profaci said. But D'Elia said there would have been ways to get around that.

"You know what they say in New York, don't you?" he asked.

"Accidents happen," replied Profaci without missing a beat.

"Oops, we didn't know," said D'Elia.

"Oops is right," repeated Profaci. "Shame on us."

But now, they told Avena, the only solution was to accept the offer that the Genovese family had worked out.

"Better to win small than to lose big," said Stanfa, clearly concerned about a clash with the larger Genovese organization. "They got all the power. They can run an army, okay?"

Piccolo, ever the voice of reason, also urged Avena to settle.

"It's no longer about Carmine Franco," said the silver-haired gentleman gangster and Avena's longtime friend. "It's about making sure no one gets hurt. . . . This could be a fuckin' tragedy."

While Avena didn't seem to realize it at the time—he kept insisting that he would win a lawsuit if it ever went to court—his legal rights and his trash business were not the only things at risk.

Two days after the D'Elia conference, Avena, Piccolo, and Stanfa were picked up discussing the situation. Avena said he knew the case "had gone further than it should have" and that the references to organized crime now scattered across the court record had become a problem. But, paraphrasing an old Sicilian proverb, he said, "You can't put the shit back in the donkey."

After Avena left the room, Stanfa and Piccolo continued to talk about the dispute. Stanfa said that Avena had to accept the settlement. "I know, John," replied Piccolo sadly. "He [Avena] don't understand."

What Avena didn't understand, but what was perfectly clear to Stanfa and Piccolo was that if Avena did not go along, he would be killed. More troubling to Stanfa and Piccolo was the possibility that either Sal Profaci or they would be ordered to carry out the hit.

"They gonna say to Sal [Profaci], 'Do this,' " Stanfa said of the New York mobsters, "or they do this."

"Or we have to do it," Piccolo added ominously.

Four months after D'Elia put the mob's cards on the table for Avena, the civil suit was settled quietly out of court. Details of the settlement were not made public at the time, but surfaced during the RICO trials that followed. Avena won a $2 million settlement. He got $200,000 up front. According to the FBI, he was still waiting for the rest of the money when he was brought to trial in February 1996.

The end of the trash dispute effectively removed Profaci and D'Elia from the stage that was Avena's law office, a sad day for FBI agents monitoring the tapes. The two mob leaders were articulate, well-spoken, and loaded with information. And, unaware of the bugs, they seemed all too happy to share it with whomever happened to be present.

La Cosa Nostra, Profaci said in one conversation, "is a beautiful way of life if we respect it."

D'Elia agreed.

"The way it's supposed to be, it's not an instrument to make money," he said.

Yet making money, anywhere, anyhow, was a topic that came up in almost every one of the mobsters' conversations.

Take the pizza and pasta tapes, for example.

Stanfa had set up his son and daughter, Joseph and Sara, in the food distribution business. Their company, Continental Imported Food Distributors, located in the Grays Ferry section of South Philadelphia, sold gourmet and upscale Italian food products to stores and restaurants in Philadelphia and its suburbs. Stanfa was listed as a salesman for the company.

Sal Profaci had been involved behind the scenes in the food distribution business since the 1970s, according to state and federal authorities. His son was involved with a New Jersey–based food distributor that Profaci referred to as "my company."

During a series of discussions late in 1992, the FBI heard how the mob "sells" its products. Profaci, it turned out, was more than a little upset when Continental began to sell cheese to local pizza shops. That's not how business was done, he told Stanfa.

"I'm in all the pizza shops," Profaci boasted. "And if I'm not there today, I will be there tomorrow."

Later, he outlined his sales technique for John and Joe Stanfa at a meeting to discuss the sale of a particular brand of imported pasta to a local supermarket chain. The Stanfas, through Continental, had begun to sell the same product to four stores in the chain at a price lower than Profaci was able to offer the stores.

Profaci said he couldn't match Stanfa's price because he had had to pay a bribe to get premium shelf space in the supermarkets for his products. He said he also paid to get certain brands of cheese well placed. As a result, his costs were higher than the Stanfas, who hadn't had to pay any bribes.

In an FBI summary report of the so-called "pasta sit-down," FBI Supervising Agent Charlotte Lang wrote:

> Stanfa's sale to the four stores at a lower price could jeopardize the entire 274-store chain to whom Profaci sells. Sal Profaci pointed out to Stanfa that the kickbacks involved in selling the chain kept Profaci from meeting Stanfa's price . . . that he had . . . to pay $65,000 to get shelf space (for the cheese products), but could not remember how much he had to pay for the shelf space [for the pasta products].

Profaci then suggested that before selling to any other supermarkets, Stanfa consult with him about the price to be charged.

"Profaci reminded Stanfa that this sort of price-fixing is illegal," Lang wrote in her report, "but that among themselves they could fix the price in advance. Avena interjected that any agreement to set a price is illegal and instructed the others that they should never admit that they had discussed prices."

A month later, the FBI bug picked up Stanfa discussing how mobsters in the same business shouldn't cut each other's throats. He said he had passed up the opportunity to sell more to the supermarket chain, despite calls from the company.

"Stanfa let the opportunity go because he did not want a misunderstanding with the Profacis," Lang wrote.

Profaci's hidden interest in the food business—like the mob's influence in the trash hauling industry—is now part of an FBI investigative file that grew out of the Avena tapes. So are several other tidbits that turned up during conversations involving D'Elia and Stanfa.

On one, D'Elia boasted that he had paid $50,000 to a Pennsylvania Department of Environmental Resources official to protect an illegal trash-dumping operation. D'Elia also said he and a former Teamsters union official were receiving a commission on all the trash Franco was dumping at an upstate Pennsylvania landfill. Another discussion alluded to the illegal dumping of asbestos after it was secretly mixed with common trash.

The feds also heard Stanfa discuss an illegal trash-dumping scheme in which, he said, he, Profaci, and D'Elia could share in a skim of "six dollars per ton" in a venture that he estimated would generate "150 tons a day." There was also talk of a bribe or tribute of $200,000 or $250,000 paid to members of the Gambino organization in order to obtain the rights to a private trash hauling contract in the South Philadelphia Italian Market area.

Federal authorities hoped the Avena tapes would be an eye-opener for that segment of the American public that often exhibited blase attitudes toward organized crime. ("Who cares about gambling. Everybody gambles. And when they kill, they only kill one another. They don't bother me, I don't bother them.")

Here, out of the mouths of the wiseguys themselves, was reason to be concerned. The cost of a slice of pizza or a box of spaghetti, the taxes paid for trash pickup at the curb and the unfathomable price of despoiling the environment through illegal and unregulated dumping practices all were tied to the mob. All were part of La Cosa Nostra's cost of doing business.

7

In the fall of 1992, with the Franco-Avena dispute finally on the way to a peaceful resolution, John Stanfa began to focus on the more immediate problem of Joey Merlino and the other "little Americans." Ultimately, he knew, he would have to kill them. So he began to plot their demise.

Stanfa had two shooters lined up and ready to go.

They were young.

They were eager.

And best of all, from Stanfa's perspective, they were Sicilian.

But then they both started making eyes at Stanfa's beautiful, twenty-four-year-old daughter, Sara, whose soft features and brooding good looks reminded them of the lemon-scented breezes and warm nights of home.

And so what started as a treacherous murder conspiracy of Machiavellian proportions degenerated into a deadly dark comedy, an underworld love triangle involving a Mafia princess and her two hapless hit men suitors. At another time and in another place it would have been the stuff of an opera by Puccini or a play by Shakespeare. But this was South Philadelphia, circa 1992.

And so it became Pulp Fiction.

Biagio Adornetto and Rosario Bellocchi first surfaced in the Stanfa investigation when they were observed working in the Warfield Breakfast and Luncheon Express in the spring of 1992. Adornetto, thirty, was seven years older and slightly taller than Bellocchi. But they were remarkably similar in several other ways. Both were thin and wiry with thick, black hair and midnight eyes. Both were new arrivals in the city. Both worked as waiters at several Italian restaurants before attracting Stanfa's attention.

Most important, both were hot-blooded and ambitious.

The Warfield was a small luncheonette located on the corner of Warfield and Wharton Streets, just up the block from Stanfa's Continental food warehouse. The property, a squat cinderblock building that housed the luncheonette and an attached storage garage, was owned by Stanfa. But the business was being run by Joe Ciancaglini Jr., who had been formally inducted into the mob in November 1991. A short time later, Stanfa named "Joey Chang" underboss.

It was considered a smart move. Joe Ciancaglini, just thirty-four, would be a bridge between Stanfa and the group of young Turks headed by Merlino and Joey Chang's brother, Mike.

After the Bocchino murder and the botched hit on Mike Ciancaglini, things had quieted down. Joey Merlino came out of prison in the spring and was spotted meeting with Stanfa both at Continental and at social functions, including a wedding in May where the FBI took nearly as many photos as the professional hired by the bride's family. That September Stanfa held another secret making ceremony. Merlino and Mike Chang were inducted into the organization, formalizing the rapprochement between the Old World mob boss and the streetcorner wiseguys. Adornetto, who was also made that day, waited until he was alone with Stanfa to ask why he was bringing the young Americans, whom he knew Stanfa despised, into the family. Stanfa told him to be patient. He intended to kill them. But for now, he wanted them close so that he could keep an eye on them and stabilize the organization.

Several others, including Piccolo and Sparacio, cautioned against making Merlino and Mike Ciancaglini. Piccolo and Sparacio had seen and survived the violence of the Scarfo years. They knew the price the organization had paid in blood and jail terms. Both felt that Merlino and his associates were too flamboyant, that they would attract too much attention, that they would try to muscle their way into business deals and that, ultimately, they would return to the confrontational style that had cost Felix Bocchino his life.

"I done things I'd a got a hundred years for now," Sparacio said in one conversation with Piccolo and Avena. "Today we got to create a whole new image. You got to get public apathy on your side, too. You got to soft soap everything. And get out of the limelight, not create a problem that gets in the limelight."

Even with the malapropism, Sparacio conveyed the sentiment of most of the older members of the organization. Public apathy and indifference were preferable to screaming newspaper headlines and nightly television broadcasts trumpeting the latest developments in the underworld. The idea was to make money, not headlines. Guys like Scarfo and Gotti had lost sight of that—and everyone knew where they ended up. Now Sparacio and Piccolo were warning Stanfa that young hotheads like Merlino and Mike Ciancaglini would take the organization back in that same direction.

At another meeting, Piccolo told Stanfa: "You can't afford to have these fellas around you, John. . . . They'll destroy everybody."

Stanfa listened, but kept his own counsel. He had a plan. Adornetto and Bellocchi, the young Sicilian hit men in waiting, would play a major part in it. They would be the backbone of the new Philadelphia mob, an organization that could trace its roots directly to Palermo. They were part of the new wave of Mafiosi that Italian magistrate Giovanni Falcone had begun tracking when he was killed. In the fall of 1992, they were perfectly positioned, ready to move up in the organization, poised to kill anyone in their way.

Adornetto may have been a lowly restaurant worker struggling to survive, but he had big plans. In talks with Bellocchi and in telephone calls home to friends and family members in Sicily, he boasted about his connections and his prospects for advancement. He was going to be a player. He was sure of it. He knew more about the ways of the Mafia than his American counterparts. He had the bloodlines and he had the balls. In fact he consistently berated Joe Ciancaglini, Stanfa's new underboss, questioning his judgment and his courage and maintaining that he—Adornetto—would be better suited for the number two spot.

"Biagio used to say Joe Chang wasn't worth it," Bellocchi recalled. "He said American people were stupid . . . stupid in a certain way. Not really smart enough to be mob members, to be in a position to lead.''

In another conversation, Adornetto confided to Bellocchi: ''We are special people. We are Sicilians. We can kill any people we want.''

It was around this time that Adornetto asked Stanfa for permission to court his daughter.

Sara, who had been born and raised in Philadelphia, was a first-generation Italian American brought up in a household that still clung to Old World values. As smart as she was beautiful, she was probably the most charismatic of Stanfa's three children. Still, she was a woman, not a man. Later the FBI would hear Stanfa lament that fact while praising the guile and gumption of his firstborn.

Following the custom of his native Sicily, Adornetto asked permission from the father to court the daughter. But Stanfa, in a rare acknowledgment of his daughter's independent streak and American roots, left the matter in Sara's hands. It would be up to her, he told Adornetto. Privately, however, Stanfa was pleased when his daughter rebuffed Adornetto, whose crude, blunt manner and arrogant style had already begun to wear thin on the mob boss.

Bellocchi, on the other hand, had a practiced naivete that was charming if somewhat contrived. When he professed his feelings for Sara, he got a green light from both the mob boss and the Mafia princess.

And so the three corners of a deadly underworld love triangle were set.

That fall, both young Sicilians were assigned to carry out hits for the Stanfa organization.

Adornetto was part of a team that was supposed to

rub out Ron Mazzone and Rod Colombo, two mob associates who were suspected of playing fast and loose with the money they collected in an extortion racket. Stanfa believed that some of the cash they were picking up—*his* money, after all—was finding its way into *their* pockets. So he decided to make an example of them.

The plan was to gun them down in the parking lot of a South Jersey restaurant where they were to meet Stanfa for dinner one night. Mazzone and Colombo showed up on time. Adornetto and his associates did not. The chance was lost and the hit was called off as soon as the two unsuspecting targets strode into the restaurant. Adornetto later blamed two other members of the hit team for botching the job, claiming they lacked the guts to carry out the assignment.

A few weeks later, Bellocchi was told by Stanfa and Joe Ciancaglini Jr. to ''take care of'' Francisco DiGiacomo, a young South Philadelphia gambler and suspected drug dealer who had been falsely and publicly bragging about his connections to the Stanfa mob.

Unlike Adornetto, Bellocchi took care of business.

DiGiacomo was one of the first friends Bellocchi had made when he arrived in South Philadelphia from Sicily in 1991. Yet he didn't hesitate when Stanfa said he wanted the man killed. One night late in November, Bellocchi took his friend out drinking. They stopped for beers at a local tavern, then headed to a popular nightclub. Later, as they were riding in a car on a deserted street near Philadelphia's old historic district, Bellocchi pulled out a gun and pumped four bullets into his friend's neck and chest.

Then he stopped the vehicle, pulled the body out of

the car, dumped it in the gutter, and drove away.

On the witness stand, the young hit man described his first mob killing this way: "I shoot the guy, I don't remember how many times. The poor guy, he was crying. He say, 'Rosario, why you do this to me?' I said, 'Don't make this any harder for me.' I shoot him. Then I got out of the car, took him out, and just left him there."

The killing pleased Stanfa and Ciancaglini, but infuriated Adornetto. Bellocchi had used a gun taken from Adornetto's home to kill DiGiacomo. He also had "borrowed" Adornetto's car to carry out the hit and had shattered a window and gotten blood all over the interior in the process. Two days later the car was disposed of by a friend of Stanfa's in the compacting business.

"Adornetto . . . wanted to kill me," Bellocchi said.

Stanfa, on the other hand, was beaming, proud that something had finally been accomplished, that someone had finally been able to carry out an assignment.

The day after the killing, Bellocchi showed up for work at the Warfield and told Ciancaglini, "You got what you wanted. The job is done." Later that day, he said, Stanfa came up to him at work, patted him on the shoulder, and said, "Don't worry about it. You done good."

Stanfa also told Bellocchi not to be concerned about Adornetto, whose bad-mouthing of Ciancaglini had gotten back to the mob boss. Bellocchi, who had clearly become the favorite of both John and Sara Stanfa, helped to further undermine his rival's standing by providing Ciancaglini and Stanfa with more details. He told them about Adornetto's disdain for Ciancaglini and about his lust for power.

As a reward for the DiGiacomo murder, Bellocchi, who had been living with Adornetto, was offered an apartment owned by one of Stanfa's relatives in South Philadelphia. After returning there from work one night, he found the place completely furnished, compliments of the mob boss.

"I have no words to say thank you," Bellocchi told Stanfa. Later he told authorities that the apartment and the furnishings were "a kind of payment for the favor I had done, the demonstration of my availability."

The DiGiacomo murder went largely unnoticed in underworld and law enforcement circles, and did not become a part of the Stanfa indictment until after Bellocchi began cooperating in 1995. At the time, November 29, 1992, it warranted no more than a three-paragraph story buried inside the city's two daily newspapers.

The victim, the papers said, was found dead on a cobblestoned street in Philadelphia's historic Old City area. DiGiacomo, twenty-two, had died of multiple gunshot wounds to the neck and chest, according to a police report. He was dressed in a blue jogging suit and white sneakers. He had a dollar in his pocket. Homicide detectives said they had no suspects and no motive. There was no mention of any mob connection.

A month later, Bellocchi, who was now courting Sara Stanfa in earnest, was asked to again "demonstrate his availability" to John Stanfa. This time the assignment was even closer to home. Stanfa wanted Bellocchi to "deliver a message" to Adornetto.

Early in December there was an electrical fire at the Warfield Express and Joe Ciancaglini was forced to shut the place down for several weeks. Adornetto, who had been picking up bad vibes, decided to use that excuse to find another job. He ended up working as a pizza maker at La Veranda, perhaps the best Italian restaurant in Philadelphia.

Located on Delaware Avenue near Spring Garden Street, the posh restaurant is a piece of Rome overlooking the Delaware River. The pasta dishes are exquisite. The steaks and chops, cooked on the same wood-fired grill where Adornetto made pizzas, are as tender and sweet as butter, and the seafood is sinfully delicious.

Every mover and shaker in the city—and anyone else who wanted to be—found their way to La Veranda for a power lunch or a sumptuous dinner. Stanfa ate there regularly, often taking a table in the back where he and an entourage of ten or twelve associates would sit for hours, sampling the antipasto misto and the buschetta, washing down an entree of pasta or veal chops with a fine wine and then lingering over dessert and espresso.

So frequent were Stanfa's visits that the mayor and other city politicos used to check with police before making a reservation in order to avoid being in the restaurant at the same time as the mob boss. Gossip columnists could have a field day playing with that juxtaposition.

Adornetto's work station was in the front of the long, narrow building, not far from the entrance and the valet parking area. He worked the dinner shift on most nights, sweating over the ovens and grills where the pizzas, breads, and rolls that were used as appetizers were prepared. It was hot, dull, stationary work.

He was a perfect target.

Even though he had left the Warfield and put some
distance between himself and the Stanfa organization,
Adornetto continued to complain about Joe Ciancaglini
to anyone who would listen. And, more to Stanfa's
dismay, he was still calling Sara Stanfa on the telephone.

This unwanted attention was apparently the last straw.

"Biagio called my daughter again," Stanfa told Bellocchi. "I'm tired of this guy. Nobody can save this guy.
This guy's gotta die."

A few days later, on December 21, 1992, FBI agents
recorded a cryptic conversation between John Stanfa and
Anthony Piccolo in the conference room of Sal Avena's
law office.

"Something cooking?" Piccolo asked.

"Something cooking," said Stanfa. "This is him.
This time . . . I don't take no fuckin' chances for nobody."

"Nah," said Piccolo.

"Believe me," said Stanfa before mumbling something that the feds could not make out.

"Kill Biagio?" asked Piccolo.

"He gotta go," said Stanfa.

"Got a date?"

"Do it tonight, or if not, tomorrow night."

"Oh, Jesus Christ."

It was supposed to be a classic mob hit carried out
with the weapon of choice of the Sicilian Mafia, a
sawed-off shotgun known as a *lupara*.

"Meester Johnny Stanfa said to me, 'You must use
the lupara,' " Bellocchi said in his thick Sicilian-
accented English. "He said it would send a message

because the Sicilian Mafia uses the lupara. He said go right in his face. Blow his head off. That way there would be no mistake.''

But this was Philadelphia, not Palermo.

The message lost something in the translation.

On the night of December 30, 1992, Rosario Bellocchi walked into La Veranda, a ski mask pulled down over his face, a sawed-off shotgun in his hands. With a getaway car idling in the valet parking area out front, the wiry, dark-haired hit man approached the pizza ovens, leveled his gun at Biagio Adornetto's head, and squeezed the trigger.

''I put the shotgun in his face and I shoot,'' Bellocchi said. ''I was surprised. The shotgun didn't go off. I shoot again. Again nothing.''

Bellocchi ran out of the restaurant, checked to make sure the gun was loaded, and ran back in. By that point Adornetto was heading for an exit at the opposite end of the building. Bellocchi, now brandishing a pistol as well as the shotgun, gave chase. Patrons scrambled for cover—the restaurant was packed—ducking under tables and hiding behind chairs. Among the crowd was a state senator, dining with some friends. He later said he had seen nothing.

''In my mind, I think he's gonna get his gun,'' Bellocchi said of the brief chase through the crowded dining room. ''With all these people around, it's gonna be a mess. He's gonna shoot me. I'm gonna shoot him. . . . So I decided to get out of there.''

Bellocchi turned and ran out of the restaurant without attempting to fire another shot. Later that night, he learned that his accomplice and getaway driver had put the wrong size shells in the shotgun, causing the *lupara* to misfire.

"He apologized," Bellocchi said. "He said not to worry. It was his fault."

The blunder was the first of many that would plague the Stanfa organization in the mob war that followed. Adornetto, who went into hiding, became the focus of an intense underworld search over the next three months, leading to a botched kidnapping attempt that was even more haphazard than the La Veranda misadventure.

Stanfa, both embarrassed and angry, railed against his bad luck and cursed the gods who were looking down with disfavor on him. Then he ordered everyone in the organization to help locate Adornetto who, he believed, may have headed to California or Italy. No matter where he was, he wanted him found. He asked for help from mobsters in New York and Sicily and told Bellocchi if Adornetto had talked with law enforcement authorities, he wanted to find him and make an example of him.

"He said he wanted to kill him, cut his penis off, put it in his mouth, and leave his body on Delaware Avenue . . . to show people he had talked too much," Bellocchi said.

A week after the bungled hit at La Veranda, police found Rod Colombo dead behind the wheel of his Cadillac, which was parked on a residential street in Audubon, a South Jersey bedroom community in the Philadelphia suburbs. Colombo, who had dodged a bullet in the restaurant parking lot two months earlier, wasn't as lucky the second time the mob got him in its sights. The musclebound mob enforcer had two bullet holes in the back of his head.

Stanfa was eventually convicted of ordering the killing, but no one has ever been charged with carrying out the hit. For a time Bellocchi was a suspect, but he had a solid alibi.

That night Bellocchi's father had flown into Kennedy Airport in New York from Palermo. Rosario had been there to pick him up. And after returning to South Philadelphia, he had gone to a party where a dozen witnesses and several photographs attested to his presence.

The night Rod Colombo was murdered, January 7, 1993, was also Rosario Bellocchi's twenty-fourth birthday.

The Stanfas threw a party for him. Coincidentally, their youngest daughter, Maria, was also born on that date. She was turning seventeen. The Stanfas had two cakes at the party that night, one covered with pink and white icing for their teenaged daughter and one covered with blue and white for the hit man who was now the love of their oldest daughter's life.

John Stanfa, who would go on at length on the FBI tapes about the importance of family and who was deeply offended by an FBI surveillance photo of Sara and Rosario kissing outside the Continental Food Warehouse, happily embraced the young man he knew to be a ruthless, cold-blooded killer, opening the doors not only to his crime family, but to his home, encouraging the romance between his daughter and his hit man.

Three weeks after the Colombo hit, another mobster turned up dead in New Jersey. Mario "Sonny" Ricco-

bene was shot and killed in the parking lot of a diner in
Brooklawn. Riccobene, the half-brother of imprisoned
Philadelphia mobster Harry "The Hump" Riccobene,
had recently returned to South Jersey after inexplicably
quitting the Witness Protection Program. Sonny Riccobene had testifed against his half-brother and several
other mob associates in a 1984 racketeering case. Why
he thought he could return was a mystery that even the
wiseguys couldn't fathom.

"For some reason he thought he was okay," said a
former Stanfa associate. In fact, the associate said, Riccobene went to meet with Stanfa, a move that shocked
the mob boss.

"John didn't know what to say. He couldn't understand it."

While no one has ever been charged with the Riccobene murder, authorities believe it was ordered by Stanfa
and carried out by several of his associates.

In addition to his young Sicilians, Stanfa had brought
several former members of Harry Riccobene's mob faction into his organization. Harry the Hump had battled
Scarfo in the early 1980s in a mob war that left a dozen
wiseguys dead or wounded. One of those who survived
a Scarfo-ordered ambush was Frank Martines, a handsome and stocky construction worker who was now part
of the Stanfa mob. Another former Riccobene associate,
Raymond Esposito, was seen regularly around Continental and was soliciting business for the food distribution company in South Jersey. Esposito brought Philip
Colletti, a lanky, dark-haired pseudo-wiseguy, into
Stanfa's orbit. Colletti, a plumber by trade, had done six
months on a manslaughter rap in 1981 after shooting a
man in a neighborhood dispute. He had been "around"
Harry Riccobene at the time and word on the street was

that Riccobene had helped grease the judicial system so that Colletti could walk away from a potential murder rap. Esposito and Colletti became part of a shakedown crew that solicited and collected extortion money for Stanfa.

With all those former associates around Stanfa, perhaps Sonny Riccobene thought he would be welcomed back, that all would be forgiven. It was a fatal miscalculation on the part of the former wiseguy. For months federal authorities watched as he moved around the fringes of the organization. He was living with his elderly mother in a rural area of South Jersey, but would pop up from time to time in South Philadelphia, often to visit a former girlfriend there.

In addition to meeting at least once with Stanfa, Sonny Riccobene apparently reestablished contact with some of his old mob associates, including Esposito. Authorities believe Riccobene, who like his jailed brother had dabbled in the methamphetamine business, was hoping to set up a few drug deals in order to generate some income.

On the evening of January 28, 1993, he went to the Brooklawn Diner for a meeting. A waiting gunman ran up to his car and opened fire. Sonny Riccobene was sixty when he died.

His passing was duly noted, but hardly mourned in the underworld.

FBI Surveillance Tape
February 1, 1993
12:33 P.M.

SALVATORE AVENA: How about Sonny?
SALVATORE SPARACIO: Yeah. Damn fool all his life.

AVENA: It's tragic the way he [unintelligible] up everything, including his family. He had that nice woman,
   Angela. I feel badly for the old lady. I know her. Do
   you know her?

SPARACIO: No.

AVENA: Really sad.

SPARACIO: It is sad. They create sadness in their life.

AVENA: Not to say, that was deserving, don't misunderstand me. But this violence . . .

SPARACIO: Well, it figures to end.

AVENA: See, Sam, you've got to build strength. Fear don't
   get you strength.

SPARACIO: No, but this doesn't hurt nothing. This one,
   anyhow.

Three days later, FBI agents again heard Avena and
Sparacio discuss the Riccobene murder. This time the
two started out commenting on a newspaper report spec-
ulating that Stanfa would be charged with ordering the
hit. Both Sparacio and Avena discussed the possibility
of informants providing information to the New Jersey
State Police. Sparacio said he thought Stanfa wasn't ex-
ercising enough caution in the way he was running the
organization.

"Between you and I, Sal, I think things are a little
loose, too many, taking in too many. . . . I'm saying it's
too loose around him [Stanfa]," Sparacio said.

Avena then asked how many people might know
about the situation, an apparent reference to the Riccobene murder.

"More than two people?" he asked.

"Shouldn't be," said Sparacio.

"If there's more than two people, then you might as
well go in the advertising business," Avena noted sarcastically.

"That's right," Sparacio replied. "Shouldn't be. Shouldn't be unless they brag about what they do. These young kids. . . . Unless you're schooled ten, fifteen, twenty years around somebody, how can you really have faith?"

8

FBI Surveillance Tape
December 1, 1992
2:23 P.M.

JOHN STANFA: We're going to start the war again. . . .
They're degenerate. In other words, for money they
do anything.
ANTHONY PICCOLO: Anything.
STANFA: They sell their own mother for money.
PICCOLO: That's right, John.

The DiGiacomo, Colombo, and Riccobene killings
were internal business matters, housecleaning. Their
deaths were not going to trigger any kind of underworld
problems. The Adornetto fiasco, while an embarrassment, was also an in-house matter from which no one
expected any serious repercussions.

Stanfa's relationship with Joey Merlino and his young
associates, however, was another matter. For several
months law enforcement authorities had watched the two
mobsters circle one another. It was clear that neither
mob leader respected the other. When they were alone,
Merlino and his young henchmen referred to Stanfa as

Mob boss John Stanfa *(left)*, accompanied by body-guard Vince Filipelli and Ron Previte, arrives for a grand jury appearance in Trenton, New Jersey.

Salvatore "Shotsie" Sparacio, the veteran mobster who cautioned against violence and later fell out of favor.

Mob underboss Joe Ciancaglini (center) during a meeting with Stanfa (left) and the late Michael Palma. FBI audio and video surveillance would later record Ciancaglini being gunned down.

Joey Merlino (*left*), Gaeton Lucibello, and the late Michael Ciancaglini taking a stroll in the spring of 1993.

John Veasey (*left*), the hitman who later became the feds' top informer, accompanies Stanfa to a meeting in South Philadelphia.

Former professional bodybuilder and Mister Universe contestant Filipelli, who became Stanfa's bodyguard.

Tommy Morrone

Filipelli *(left)* and acting underboss Frank Martines in front of Stanfa's Continental Imported Food Distributors warehouse in South Philadelphia.

Martines *(left)* and Vincent "Al Pajamas" Pagano leave Stanfa's warehouse in December 1993.

Hitman Sergio Battaglia at the
entrance of Stanfa's warehouse.

Stanfa (center)
and Battaglia
chat outside
the warehouse.

Merlino associates Steve Mazzone *(left)*, Scafidi, and George Borgesi on a cold street corner. Scafidi would later switch sides in the mob war, aligning with Stanfa against his boyhood friends.

Merlino in his South Philadelphia coffee shop with television news photographer Brad Nau.

"the greaseball" and to those around him as "the greasers." At the same time, the FBI heard Stanfa, Piccolo, Sparacio, and the others complain about the Merlino group. They were loud and boisterous, said the veteran mobsters. They were bullies. They had no class.

Everyone knew it was just a matter of time before the uneasy alliance fell apart, before the bridge that Joe Ciancaglini Jr. was providing would give way under the weight of the two rival mob factions. From the beginning everyone assumed that it would be Stanfa, older, wiser, and with support from both New York and Sicily, who would prevail.

Like Stanfa, the authorities underestimated Joey Merlino. They described him as a punk, a hothead, a lowlife. But in certain underworld circles—more, in fact, than the police or Stanfa could imagine—Merlino was both feared and admired for his guts and swagger.

He had panache, a kind of streetcorner style that played well in the neighborhood. Around Christmastime, for example, while Stanfa and Piccolo were plotting his demise, Merlino decided out of the blue to host a party at a South Philadelphia beauty salon where he and several of his associates went for weekly manicures. Merlino was fanatical about his appearance and kept regular appointments with a hairstylist and a manicurist. Even later, when he was being stalked and was laying low, he would arrange for the manicurist to come to his home. Once the woman did the nails of five gangsters at Merlino's house while Stanfa gunmen were cruising the streets looking for them.

For the young wiseguys, appearance was always important.

It was a South Philly thing.

For the Christmas party, Merlino took over the beauty salon, arranging for a friend in the catering business to put out a spread—lobster, clams casino, shrimp, veal piccante, cheeses, fruits, breads, desserts. All day long customers who came in were invited to join the feast, to partake of the holiday good cheer.

At one point several eight- or nine-year-old black girls from a nearby neighborhood drifted in and began eyeing the food. The owner of the shop saw them and started making up platters for them. Then Merlino stepped in.

"What are you doin'?" he said to the beautician, who was taken aback. "That's not the way it's done. It's Christmas."

And with that, Merlino pulled a wad of cash from his pocket and proceeded to hand each little girl a twenty-dollar bill to go along with the steaming lobster, veal, and shrimp that had been piled high on their plates.

"This is how it's done," Merlino said smiling as he told each girl, "Now go and buy your mother a nice Christmas present."

"You gotta understand about Joey," said a former associate who testified against him in the armored truck heist. "If he has five thousand dollars in his pocket, he's gonna spend five thousand dollars. Money don't mean nothing to him."

As 1992 drew to a close, Merlino, who had spent more than two years in jail, was back in business, larger than life and anxious to make up for lost time. He and his entourage of macho young wiseguys used to go out every weekend to the hot new clubs that had opened along the Delaware River waterfront. Young, single, and looking to get laid, they'd pull up in two or three late-model sports cars dressed in the latest Armani or Versace fashions, their hair coiffed, their nails manicured and buffed. Lines would part. Cover charges would be waived. And here would be Joey and his guys escorted to the best table, given the best seats at the bar, attended to by a bevy of waitresses who laughed and smiled while patrons gawked and whispered, "That's him. That's Merlino. Skinny Joey."

Even without the celebrity that surrounded him, Merlino would have been the center of attention. With his piercing eyes and cockeyed smile, he was a magnet for women looking to be bad and for guys who thought they were.

"All he cares about," said an underworld source, "is bettin' and broads. He ain't afraid of going to jail. He ain't afraid of dying. He just wants to have a good time."

This, of course, was not the way Stanfa thought a wiseguy should act.

STANFA: See, it's no use. This kid, believe me, they don't belong near us. The other day somebody told me, they thought it was Saturday, Saturday night, Friday night or Saturday night, they went to a club. They say they have . . . girl, champagne, all kind of champagne, I think. And then, you know, in other words, how are you gonna show people like this? In other words, you want to party? . . . Party private.

ANTHONY PICCOLO: Sure. Get a room someplace. Sure.

STANFA: But get a . . . get a room. Get someplace in other words, you know, when you do something sharp like that, people they gotta see. See and they shaking down this, and they shaking down that. And they party, you know. In other words, you understand?

PICCOLO: John, John, you gotta use your head . . .

(*Later*)

STANFA: Believe me Tony, us people, not too many left.

PICCOLO: That's what I was telling Sal.

STANFA: These people, they're headache, they're headache.

PICCOLO: They do what they want to do.

(*Later*)

PICCOLO: John, you got, you gotta use your head here, John. You can't, John, you can't afford to have these fellas ruin you, John.

STANFA: But what am I gonna do? What am I supposed to do?

PICCOLO: We have to do what we have to do. . . . I know what they can do, John. If they don't listen, they'll destroy everybody . . . and they'll put everybody in the goddamn thing. . . . Who would be the boss?

STANFA: Tony, I don't know. . . . See, I get up every morning at five o'clock. I go work . . . and I work all the time. You know, I don't go to club. I don't go to this. I don't go to that.

PICCOLO: John, you're the only person I could think of that had sense to say, "This is a reasonable person. He knows what to do." These other guys, John, forget about them. A bunch of young Turks. And that guy [Merlino] acts like the leader. He acts like the leader.

Stanfa then said that Joe Ciancaglini, his underboss, had been receiving complaints from gamblers who had bet and won with members of the Merlino group and who said they weren't being paid. Stanfa admitted that his knowledge of sports betting was limited, but he said he knew enough to know that "you gotta have to back it up, because when you lose, you gotta pay."

"Sure and it's reputation," said Piccolo.

But Stanfa said trying to reason with Merlino and his associates was "like I talk with the wall."

PICCOLO: Crazy. Crazy John. Crazy, crazy. Damn shame. It'd be so nice.

STANFA: That's right. . . . I tried to, you know what I mean, and thank God, so far, so good. But see, this is what bothers me.

PICCOLO: You see the writing on the wall.

STANFA: You know, I try to put wood on the fire and then somebody come in from behind and boom, and cart away the wood.

PICCOLO: Damn shame. Hey John, there's nothing you can do. They're not going to listen.

STANFA: They don't want to listen. They all, they all, they listen is, in other words, you gotta touch . . . because Tony, believe me, I told already more than one time what I do . . .

PICCOLO: They do not have discipline.

STANFA: Yeah.

PICCOLO: They don't have it. You try, you tried hard. You tried . . . in the old country.

(Later)

PICCOLO: But I worry about you, if I can talk John. But I'm gonna talk like the street. I don't give a fuck about them, John. I worry about you, because I know what they are, John. I know they ain't gonna change. . . . They showed that time and time again. But you, I don't want you to have to pay for their sins.

STANFA: You tell me what you got in mind. You know what I mean. So?

PICCOLO: Like this. They're gonna hurt you, John. They're never beaten. At least one . . . that guy you gotta . . .

STANFA: See, Tony, I get, I go along with you all the way. See this . . . stinks. This, see we do that guy, we're gonna start the war.

PICCOLO: Nah.

STANFA: I'll tell you.

PICCOLO: You think so, don't you?

STANFA: I know. See Tony, in other words, I go along with you. I agree with you a hundred percent. But I

know. See, you don't see what I see. . . . The problem
is, we gonna start, you know, we gonna give satisfaction we start to kill each other.

PICCOLO: John, it's better them than us.

(Later)

STANFA: I say we . . . gotta go slowly, slowly, because we
got a good future . . . in front of us.

PICCOLO: What, are you kidding John? Sure.

STANFA: And they want to choke it. 'Ats why, no even
that. See, their problem, what they real main problem
is what I see it, see, they got a hundred, they spend
two hundred. See, they got a thousand, they spend two
thousand . . .

PICCOLO: Two thousand.

STANFA: . . . because they too show off. Because they figure it's easy come and easy go. And then they, they
choking because they broke, and they do anything, in
other words they forget about it. . . . That's what
they're doing.

PICCOLO: Exactly right, John. You're right, hundred percent.

Two months after recording the highly incriminating
conversation in which Stanfa and Piccolo discussed going to war with the Merlino faction, the FBI's black bag
squad was at it again.

After obtaining court authorization, agents broke into
the Warfield Breakfast and Luncheon Express and
planted a microphone. The feds also mounted a camera
on a pole about a block away and had it trained on the
front of the building. The audio and video was beamed
back to a surveillance post about a mile away where an
agent was assigned each day to monitor comings and
goings.

Stanfa was meeting with some of his top associates
on a regular basis in the Warfield, but for the first few

weeks, very little of importance was picked up. Most of their conversations were whispered in the back of the shop or in the adjacent storage garage, out of range of the bugs and the camera.

On the morning of March 2, things changed.

Paul Hayes Jr., the FBI agent on loan from the bureau's Sicilian squad to work the Stanfa case, had drawn monitoring duty. It was supposed to be a routine surveillance, another one of those tedious days watching and listening.

Shortly before six A.M. Hayes, seated in front of a television screen, watched Joe Ciancaglini go through the daily ritual of opening his shop for business.

With the video screen programmed to tick off the date, hour, minute, and second, Hayes saw Ciancaglini and Susan Lucibello, who worked as a waitress, pull up in a car in front of the luncheonette at 5:57 A.M. As the seconds ticked off, the screen showed Ciancaglini and Lucibello getting out of the car. Ciancaglini released the burglar grate that covered the front entrance, unlocked the door, entered the building, and turned on the lights.

Susan Lucibello followed him in.

For several more seconds they could be seen moving around inside the building, their shadows darting across the lighted restaurant in the predawn hour.

Then a dark, four-door sedan passed across the television screen from right to left, pulling down Wharton Street onto Warfield and offscreen. Seconds later three dark figures appeared from the left of the screen, running through the front door of the restaurant.

Hayes scanned the monitor. Then he heard Susan Lucibello scream. Next came a staccato round of seven or eight shots. Another scream. More gunfire. Then the sound of footsteps as the three gunmen ran out the front door and disappeared the way they had come.

Hayes, a mile away, called FBI headquarters, then dialed 9-1-1. In less than a minute he was in his own car, speeding toward the luncheonette. He got there in five minutes. Police were already on the scene. Joey Ciancaglini, shot repeatedly in the head, neck, and chest, was lying in a pool of blood. Moments later he was on an emergency squad stretcher being rushed to a hospital.

The FBI had it all on film.

It was the rarest of all surveillance tapes and one that would mesmerize the jury in the Stanfa trial.

It was a mob hit in progress.

In the weeks that followed, FBI agents and detectives with the Philadelphia police department watched the tape again and again. Attempts to enhance the video—to bring up the shadowy figures, to determine the make, color, or license plate number of the car—proved unsuccessful. Had the hit gone off a half hour later, after the sun had come up and the street was awash with natural light, the enhancement might have paid off. Instead, the video was a tantalizing piece of evidence that took authorities nowhere.

"It was just too dark," said Hayes.

Miraculously, Joe Ciancaglini survived, but he never fully recovered. Both his hearing and his vision were permanently impaired. The bones in his face were shattered and had to be reconstructed. For months after finally leaving the hospital, he walked with a cane. He was a thirty-five-year-old Mafia cripple, no longer an active member of the organization.

And no longer the bridge between John Stanfa and Joey Merlino.

Speculation about the source of the Ciancaglini shooting spread quickly through both underworld and law enforcement circles. There were two active theories. One pointed toward Biagio Adornetto. Several members of the Stanfa organization thought the young Sicilian was taking his revenge for the attempt on his own life at La Veranda. Everyone knew he detested Ciancaglini and knew he had a motive for trying to take him out.

Within hours of the shooting, Sparacio and Avena were heard gossiping about the hit in Avena's office. Avena was convinced it had come from "the wrong side of the street."

"Thin Joey?" Avena asked, referring to Skinny Joey Merlino.

"No . . . it can't be here," Sparacio said, certain that the shooting was ordered from somewhere outside the city.

A day later, Avena and Piccolo talked about the hit again. This time, Piccolo mentioned Adornetto.

"I didn't know that Biagio was threatened, the thing with the shotgun," Avena said.

"He got cute with John's daughter," Piccolo said knowingly.

"Biagio?" asked Avena. "Made a pass at his daughter?"

The other theory was that the Joe Ciancaglini shooting was the work of the Merlino faction, a position that both the FBI and Stanfa eventually adopted.

"I talked to Biagio right after the shooting," Hayes said later. "I had seen a pickup truck like his down around the Warfield when Joey Chang got shot and so I went to see him.''

Well-dressed, well-spoken, and able to converse in both English and Italian, Hayes had developed a rapport with many of the wiseguys he was tracking and was able to confront Adornetto about the Ciancaglini hit without spooking the young mobster.

Adornetto's response, Hayes said, convinced him that he had nothing to do with the shooting.

''If you're gonna kill a snake, you cut off its head,'' Adornetto told Hayes. ''I would have shot Stanfa.''

Then, he calmly added, ''I would have used the *lupara*,'' an obvious reference to the sawed-off shotgun Bellocchi had had that night in La Veranda. ''And the message would have been, 'Mine works.' ''

It was an interesting conversation and it left Hayes certain of two things: Biagio Adornetto was not involved in the Joey Chang hit and Biagio Adornetto was a source worth cultivating.

Stanfa, like the FBI, eventually came to believe that Merlino and his associates were behind the hit on Joey Ciancaglini. But for several weeks after the shooting, Adornetto was a prime suspect. As a result, Stanfa ordered his men to pull out all the stops in their search for the elusive pizza man. This, in turn, led to another classic underworld blunder.

Bellocchi and a mob associate, Gary Tavella, had, on Stanfa's orders, tried to kidnap a waiter who was a friend of Adornetto's and who, Stanfa believed, might know where Adornetto was hiding.

Stanfa planned to torture the information out of the young waiter, Fernando Vincenti, by tying him in a chair and systematically cutting off his fingers with a hatchet. If Vincenti refused to disclose where Adornetto was, the mob boss said, he'd be killed.

And if he didn't know, Bellocchi asked?

Then it would be too late, Stanfa replied, and they'd have to kill him anyway.

Fernando Vincenti left his job at the San Marco Restaurant on City Avenue a little after ten P.M. on Friday night, March 19, 1993. He had started the engine to his car that cold night and then felt the call of nature. He was, police later reported, urinating against a tree when Bellocchi and Tavella, who had been waiting, pulled up in a van.

Like the hit on Adornetto at La Veranda, the kidnapping of Fernando Vincenti was a high profile failure. Several other employees, leaving work at the same time, saw Vincenti forced into the van at gunpoint. Two ran out onto City Avenue and waved frantically at a Philadelphia police patrol car parked across the street. Moments later when the van, with Tavella behind the wheel, screeched out of the parking lot and onto City Avenue, the patrol car, its siren wailing, its red lights flashing, gave pursuit.

It was a car chase right out of the movies.

City Avenue is a four-lane highway that is the boundary line between the City of Philadelphia and a string of upscale suburban communities like Bala Cynwyd and Lower Merion. It is lined with bars, restaurants, hotels, the studios of two of the city's television stations, and several high-priced department stores like Saks and Bonwit Teller. On most Friday nights it is clogged with traffic.

The night Vincenti was snatched was no exception.

Tavella gunned the engine of the dilapidated Ford van he was driving, hitting seventy and eighty miles an hour, crisscrossing lanes and swerving around vehicles. At one point he rode up on the sidewalk. Back on the street, he sideswiped a bus, then crossed over into the oncoming lane, and drove several other cars coming in the opposite direction off the road. A mile from the restaurant parking lot, he turned onto the Schuylkill Expressway heading toward Philadelphia. The patrol car was still in hot pursuit and had radioed a call for assistance that brought several other police cars to the area.

Vincenti was bouncing around in the back of the van. Tavella and Bellocchi were looking at each other nervously.

They both smelled smoke.

"The engine died," Bellocchi explained sheepishly. "Coupla miles ahead, it just died. There was smoke coming out. I said to Gary, 'You burned out the engine.' "

Bellocchi had the presence of mind to throw the .38 caliber pistol and the hatchet he was carrying out the window. They were recovered by police several days later along the side of the highway about a mile from where the van eventually stopped. Another gun was discovered under the front seat, however.

The first cops arriving on the scene ordered all three men out of the van and placed them in the back of a police vehicle. Later, the witnesses from the San Marco, brought to the scene, explained that their friend Vincenti was an innocent victim and he was taken out of the car. But in the few minutes they were together, Bellocchi, speaking in Italian, told Vincenti that if he knew what was good for him, he'd go along with the story he was about to tell.

"I told him I was sorry and that I don't believe he knows where Biagio is," Bellocchi said. "And I told him to tell the police that this was all a fight over a girl, tell them that we had an argument at the Monte Carlo (a popular Philadelphia nightclub) two or three months ago and we are fighting."

Vincenti, deciding quickly that his options were limited, blurted out to Bellocchi that all he wanted to do was go back home to Italy. He had already made plans to leave at the end of the month.

"I told him, 'You better off,' " Bellocchi said.

Asked on the witness stand if there had, in fact, been a dispute between himself and Vincenti over a girl, Bellocchi smiled. "No," he said. "It was a piece of cake. The guy was so afraid of me." Besides, Bellocchi said, "I could never fool around with any girl there."

Ten days before the kidnapping attempt, he explained, he had become engaged to marry Sara Stanfa.

Initially, Bellocchi and Tavella were charged with kidnapping and weapons offenses. As the case wound through the preliminary hearing stages, however, it was clear authorities would have a problem with their key witness.

Vincenti gave a fractured account of his abduction, insisting at one point that he simply "went for a ride" with his good friend, Rosario Bellocchi. He was, however, hard-pressed to explain why he did this while leaving his own car door open and the engine running. He was held briefly as a material witness, then released. Within days, Fernando Vincenti was in Galipolli, Italy, a small seaport town in the southernmost part of the country.

Tavella, who owned a small variety store and was a lifelong South Philadelphia resident, was released on a personal recognizance bond a day after the incident. But for Bellocchi bail was set at $250,000. He was, authorities determined, an illegal alien. His vistor's visa had expired. New Jersey authorities, it was also disclosed at the time, considered him a suspect in the murder of Rod Colombo. (The charge was later dropped, however.)

He had been engaged to marry the boss's daughter for less than two weeks and now Rosario Bellocchi sat bewildered and angry in jail. Meanwhile, the FBI got the entire story from a series of conversations picked up in Avena's office.

Three days after the arrests, Tavella met with Avena and Luigi "Gino" Tripodi, a local restaurateur believed by the FBI to be a capo in the Stanfa crime family. During the meeting, Tavella provided a blow-by-blow account of the abduction for both those sitting in the law office and those listening a block away. He insisted that Vincenti would not testify against them and that the case would amount to nothing.

On another tape, Avena and Piccolo discussed Tavella's reliability and suspiciously questioned why he had been released while Bellocchi was still behind bars. Fear of informants was rampant within the organization. Avena and Piccolo knew the feds were always trying to make deals. In an earlier discussion, Avena had noted sarcastically, "There's always free cheese in the mousetrap."

Both said they were skeptical of Tavella, a position

that would later prove ironic. Tavella was indicted along with Stanfa, Bellocchi, and twenty-two other mob figures in March 1994. He eventually pleaded guilty to a racketeering count, admitting his role in the abduction of Vincenti. But he never cooperated with authorities. Bellocchi, on the other hand, became just what Avena and Piccolo feared, a government witness.

It was just another example of the poor character judgment that plagued the organization. Stanfa would rant and rave about the lack of "qualified" people for La Cosa Nostra, about how he wanted "quality, not quantity," yet a half dozen of those he handpicked for the mob—including the Sicilian-born hit man who was engaged to marry his daughter—became rats for the government, greedily grabbing for the free cheese.

Sparacio, who had had his differences with Stanfa in the past, was the first to voice concern. In one discussion, Piccolo talked about what a "bad break" the arrest of Bellocchi and Tavella had been.

Shotsie didn't see it that way.

"It's all we needed," he said. "That's another nail in the coffin. . . . Just when we thought we had everything smooth, fucking morons like this do this shit. It's bad for everybody."

In another conversation, he and Avena talked about the possible repercussions, including indictments, that might flow from the incident.

FBI Surveillance Tape
April 13, 1993
12:20 P.M.

SALVATORE AVENA: Lot of messed up situations.
SALVATORE SPARACIO: Yes it is. Lot of mistakes.

AVENA: Strong rumor, there's going to be some indictments coming down.

SPARACIO: It ain't good. The whole thing was a mess. Lot of people are uncomfortable.

AVENA: With this? Yeah, I don't know, Sam. What more can he [Stanfa] do? He's trying.

SPARACIO: Yeah. Just not knowledgeable about things. People vouch for people and that's a bad thing to do. That whole thing was stupid. Should never have happened.

AVENA: You mean the thing at the restaurant?

SPARACIO: . . . might cause serious consequences for them, for him . . . don't know . . . if there's ways out of it or not or is it gonna bounce in somebody's face.

Sparacio, Piccolo and several others were upset with the abduction, not only because it had gone badly, but also because it was unnecessary. Clearly, Fernando Vincenti had no idea where Adornetto was. The kidnapping was a fruitless exercise that ended with the arrests of Tavella and Bellocchi.

Although not generally known at the time, there was another, more damaging result. The botched abduction and the attendant media coverage pushed Adornetto into the arms of the feds. Convinced that he could no longer dodge and weave on the streets, he contacted the FBI and began negotiating a cooperating agreement. He became the first in what would be a long line of Stanfa crime family members to turn informant, continuing an embarrassing Philadelphia underworld tradition.

In the City of Brotherly Love, *omertà* was like the Liberty Bell, cracked and inoperative.

Even more to the point, however, Stanfa, Tripodi, Piccolo, and the others now believed the March 2 hit on Joe Ciancaglini was not the work of Adornetto, but rather an ambush set in motion and carried out by Joey Merlino and his young associates.

No one has ever been charged with the attempted murder of Joe Ciancaglini, but the FBI tapes eventually made it clear that Stanfa believed that Merlino and Michael Ciancaglini were behind the shooting, that one brother set out to kill another.

He also believed that Gaeton Lucibello, whose wife worked at the Warfield, had switched his allegiance to the young mobsters and had helped set up the hit.

What's more, Stanfa—and some well placed law enforcement authorities—believed Merlino had strong support from other underworld factions. Stanfa was convinced that high-ranking members of the Scarfo organization—Joe Ciancaglini Sr. and Merlino's father, Salvatore, both jailed on racketeering charges—were advising the Young Turks. He also learned that while in prison for the armored truck robbery, Joey Merlino had been the cellmate of Ralph Natale, a sixty-four-year-old veteran Bruno family member doing time for arson and drug trafficking. Natale was to be paroled in two years and was a potential Stanfa rival.

More troubling were hints that Natale had developed ties in prison with New York mob figures who would be happy to see Stanfa out of the picture in Philadelphia. It was speculated that the Genovese organization, through Natale, might be backing Merlino's move. Already angered over Stanfa's perceived meddling in the Avena-Franco trash dispute, members of that powerful crime family were masters of the double- and triple-cross. They had been the behind-the-scenes players in the 1980 assassination of Angelo Bruno that destabilized the Philadelphia mob. Now, more than a decade later, the theory went, they were completing the job, maneuvering to place their own proxy in charge.

On April 16, the feds heard Tripodi and Piccolo discuss the latest underworld rumor.

"Mike [Ciancaglini] and Joe Merlino are gonna kill me and John," Tripodi said.

"Oh yeah?" Piccolo asked nervously. "I didn't hear that, but I heard something else."

"They plan to kill me first," said Tripodi.

"Watch yourself," said Piccolo. "Be careful. . . . Sons of bitches, I knew it was going to come to that."

In a conversation with Avena a few days later, Piccolo again blasted the Merlino group.

"What can I tell you Sal," said the wizened and weary old mobster. "You're dealing with cowboys. . . . These are not rational people."

"The thin one's crazy," said Avena, an apparent reference to Joey Merlino.

"Right, Sal. That's what I'm saying. When is this going to stop?"

And in another conversation, Piccolo and Avena gossiped about the riff within the Ciancaglini family, the antagonism between brothers Michael and Joe Jr., and the role their imprisoned father may have played in the dispute.

FBI Surveillance Tape
April 21, 1993
2:27 P.M.

AVENA: They don't communicate at all, the two brothers?
PICCOLO: From what I understand.

AVENA: And the father's done nothing?

PICCOLO: He joined the other side.

AVENA: So he's against his one son.

PICCOLO: And John. I don't know what to tell you, Sal. And the worst part, there's no reason for it, you know? Like, if there was a reason, you try to make an excuse for somebody. Nothing, absolutely nothing.

AVENA: Did the brother [Mike Ciancaglini] have a hand in that [the shooting of Joe Ciancaglini] would you say? [Brief pause] He did?

A week later, the tapes being made in the basement a block from Avena's law office started to fill with talk of a mob war. Piccolo warned Avena that Stanfa would have to act soon.

"They better do something fast," he said. "I mean it's out in the open."

And Stanfa complained about constantly looking over his shoulder. "I can't live that way," he said, explaining that he even feared visiting Joey Ciancaglini in the hospital because he thought he might be trapped in an elevator and ambushed by Merlino gunmen.

On April 29, the feds heard the chilling conversation between Stanfa and Sergio Battaglia that authorities later used in the opening of the racketeering trial. It included Stanfa's plans to lure Merlino, Michael Ciancaglini, and Gaeton Lucibello to a still unopened restaurant for a meeting. It would be described to them as a sit-down to rearrange the organization. Mobsters from Newark and from South Jersey would be invited in order to put the Young Turks at ease. Stanfa said he might even propose promoting Joey Merlino or Mike Chang in order to keep them off guard.

But the real purpose for the sitdown was abundantly

clear from the rest of the conversation: the talk of one behind the ear; the discussion of quick-drying cement; the boast about cutting out Lucibello's tongue, putting it in an envelope and sending it to his wife.

A day later, Stanfa laid the same plan out for Piccolo and Sparacio and again the tapes were rolling.

"From Mister Nice Guy, I'm gonna be Mister Bad Guy," Stanfa said. "Today, maybe it's the times. You can do no more with these guys. . . . These people, they think of one thing."

"That's right," said Piccolo.

"No respect," said Stanfa. "Nothing. . . . They no have a respect for you, your family, anybody . . . no respect at all."

Piccolo then explained to Sparacio why it was important that he and people like Joe "Scoops" Licata from Newark show up for the meeting.

"In other words," he told Sparacio, "what he's [Stanfa] got to do is try and make these guys comfortable. Now if they knew you and Scoops are gonna be there . . . now, they're comfortable."

Piccolo also emphasized that Stanfa was not the only one at risk in the battle with Merlino. "All of us, not just him," he said. "They could take us all out."

It is FBI policy to warn any target of a potential hit, regardless of who that individual is. John Gotti, in fact, had once gotten a visit from two agents after a bug in a North Jersey restaurant revealed a plot by leaders of the Genovese organization to whack him. Gotti smirked at the feds, but privately took the warning to heart.

Early in May of 1993, Joe Merlino, Mike Ciancaglini, and Gaeton Lucibello each received a visit from the FBI.

Each was told that authorities had learned of a murder plot on his life. No other details were provided, although each was told if they had anything to say, the FBI would be happy to listen.

Like Gotti, the young mobsters did the tough guy routine. But like Gotti, they took the message seriously. The meeting Stanfa had planned never took place. Merlino, Ciancaglini, and Lucibello had no intention of sitting down anywhere with John Stanfa.

9

FBI Surveillance Tape
May 27, 1993
11:42 P.M.

SALVATORE SPARACIO: It's over. Seems like it's just over. . . . You got wild sons-of-bitches like this that are gonna destroy it all together, that gonna eat, gonna eat up everybody. Even us.
ANTHONY PICCOLO: They want to eat everybody starting with us.

John Stanfa was about to go to war, but he wasn't sure who would follow him into battle. He had decided to make a move against Merlino and Mike Ciancaglini, whom he referred to repeatedly as "animals" and "cuckolds."

Fed up with their arrogance, frustrated by their lack of respect, and embarrassed by their actions, Stanfa decided they had to go. Reports kept coming back to the mob boss about the way the Merlino crew was shaking down anyone with money, demanding payments, mocking Stanfa, and generally living the high life of the 1990s gangster—embracing the get-it-all, take-no-prisoners philosophy that had prevailed during the Scarfo era in

Philadelphia and under Gotti in New York.

"It's a different world," a frustrated Stanfa said to Avena in a conversation recorded in May 1993. "People today change like night and day. No respect no more. You can deal with nobody no more. You can trust nobody. I don't know what we coming to."

"It's true," said Avena. "It's treachery."

As time passed, Stanfa became more convinced than ever that Ralph Natale, from prison, and the Genovese family, from New York, were backing Merlino's move against him. Whether that was the case is still a matter of speculation in both law enforcement and underworld circles. What is clear is that Natale, Merlino, and the Genovese organization all benefited from the mob war that followed.

In a series of conversations, FBI agents heard Piccolo and Avena urge Stanfa to get tough. And they heard Stanfa agonize over where things might lead.

Among other things, Stanfa said, he was concerned for the safety of his son, Joe, accurately predicting that he would eventually become a target. Stanfa also said he was sorry that his older daughter, Sara, had to be exposed to all the problems and, more important, that she was in no position—being a woman—to deal with them.

Joe Stanfa, then twenty-three, was naive, Stanfa said. He had apparently been unable to see Merlino and the others for what they were. Sara, twenty-six, was smarter than her brother and saw things clearly.

"My kid, my son, you know the poor kid, he's . . . hundred percent," Stanfa told Avena during a conversation recorded on May 21, "because he knew I open up his eyes a little, and we talked, you know.

"I felt bad because . . . maybe they don't get at me, you know, they go and kill the kid, you know?

"So in the meantime, my daughter she working with me, too. . . . Sal, I wish she was a boy. Because she's intelligent, smart, and she no take no baloney from nobody. And special, see . . . how they acted and she hated their guts, you know. The other day, you know what she told me, she said, 'Daddy . . . I gonna spit in their faces.' "

In another conversation, the FBI heard Piccolo advise Stanfa to "go in nice and quiet, do a job, and leave." Avena, in two other conversations, suggested that Stanfa use "the whip" or "the broom" to straighten out the Merlino faction. Although Avena would later explain that he was urging Stanfa to instill some discipline into the organization, the feds were convinced he was counseling violence.

They all agreed that there was no point in trying to reason with Merlino.

"That guy's crazy," Avena said. "He's capable of anything."

"Yeah, I know it's useless," Stanfa replied in Sicilian. "When one is born round, he can't die square."

Avena, once again waxing philosophical, agreed.

"When you're a dwarf, they could put you on a high mountain, you're still a dwarf," the lawyer said.

But it wasn't just the Merlino crew that caused Stanfa concern. He had questions about his own people. Luigi Tripodi had taken off to Italy, supposedly to visit his mother and sisters who lived in a tiny village in Calabria. Stanfa thought Tripodi was using that as an excuse to get out of town, that he had turned tail. Raymond Esposito, another member of the organization, was constantly complaining of heart trouble. And Shotsie Sparacio, Stanfa said on more than one occasion, was little more than a bookmaker and could not be depended on to do anything of substance.

"Things look worse and worse every day," Stanfa told Piccolo during one meeting. "I don't know what I gotta do. I'm by myself."

In another conversation with Avena, he questioned the character of American mobsters in general while mocking Esposito for using the same excuse whenever he was asked to do something.

"You know, he keep saying, 'Oh my heart. Oh, I taking medicine. Oh this. Oh . . . ' " Stanfa said. "But, I tell you, Sal. . . . Believe me . . . I born and raised in this thing, alright. And I wanna die in this thing. But with the right people. Over here . . . we got a kindergarten."

Federal agents listening to the conversation could not have agreed more. It was a kindergarten. The gang that couldn't shoot straight? This gang couldn't even get off a shot. Through the early summer of 1993, Merlino and his top associates were targeted time and again by members of the Stanfa organization. And time and again they walked away unscathed.

Frank Martines, the acting underboss, was coordinating the street-level strategy. He had put together a group of young guns who were supposed to set up and ambush Skinny Joey and his top associates.

Phil Colletti, who had worked in a shakedown crew with Esposito, was brought in as a hit man, the first of several moves that would come back to haunt the crime family. Colletti's involvement with the mob and the subsequent role his wife Brenda, a former go-go dancer, would play in the underworld power struggle came to epitomize all that was wrong with the Stanfa organization.

Born and raised in South Philadelphia, Colletti, thirty-three, was living with his wife and their young son, Paulie, in South Jersey at the time. He was working as a plumber, struggling to make ends meet, but he had another career in mind. He didn't want to fix toilets and clean drains. He wanted to be a wiseguy.

Tall and reed-thin, with thick black hair and a perpetual smirk, Colletti was ready to prove how tough he was. He had earned a few bucks helping Esposito collect some extortion payments for the Stanfa organization in 1992, a move that established him as part of the Stanfa group and made him a target of the Merlino faction when the war broke out.

Brenda Colletti, a shapely redhead who looked like pop singer Bonnie Raitt, had danced in go-go bars and adult bookstores before she met Philip. She went back to work as a dancer briefly after their marriage to help earn enough money for a down payment on their house in suburban Glassboro, New Jersey, but when the trouble started she was basically a housewife and mother.

Later she would willingly talk about her involvement with the Stanfa crime family, about her dealings with the mob boss himself, about how she took a gun rap for her husband and even got involved in a bizarre plot to kill Skinny Joey. But she always shied away from talk about her days as a dancer.

She thought it made her look cheap and sleazy.

In the summer of 1993, when the trouble with Merlino started, Esposito arranged a meeting with Phil Colletti.

"Raymond told me I was on a hit list," Phil Colletti later explained. "He said because I had helped him out before, I was considered with Stanfa and that Merlino and his guys were going to come after me. Raymond asked if I would help out. He said he knew I'd rather be the hunter than the hunted."

Colletti quickly signed on. He saw it as a chance for advancement and as an opportunity to make some real money. He got most of his assignments from Martines and was put in a crew that included Martines's cousin, Salvatore Brunetti. Brunetti was short and thin with thick, dark hair, a miniature version of Colletti. They were a Mutt-and-Jeff hit team. The Collettis quickly nicknamed Brunetti "Twitch" because he was always fidgeting with things and because he could not sit still.

"If he had a gun, he'd have to take it apart and put it back together," Brenda Colletti said. "He'd take the bullets out and then put them back in. Always playing. Always touching. . . . Philip used to worry about fingerprints cause Twitch hadda touch everything, all the bullets, all the pieces of the gun."

Sergio Battaglia and his friend, Herbie Keller, a former high school classmate, rounded out the crew.

During that summer they showed up frequently at Colletti's home in Glassboro. They'd go over their plans, talk about their assignments.

"They'd be sittin' at the kitchen table talkin'," said Brenda. "And I'd be cooking for them or making coffee or making sandwiches. They talked right in front of me. I knew everything that was going on. Eventually, you get used to it, you think nothing of it. It was like we were in a war and I started to think just like they did. We hadda do what we hadda do. We had to get Merlino and his guys. We hadda get them before they got us.''

While several people involved in the mob war would later try, like Brenda Colletti, to put some kind of noble spin on the violence that followed, the feds listening to Stanfa's conversations in Avena's office knew better.

The brutal battle that opened with the ambush on Joey Ciancaglini in March was a grab for power and control. It was rooted in treachery, and it was fueled by greed and paranoia. As the agents heard when Stanfa's May 27, 1993, conversation with Piccolo and Sparacio continued:

JOHN STANFA: What we do, you know. What you say, you know, I can see it. I got, in other words, see, I gotta do more. What I'm supposed to do over here. Right now, I don't eat. I don't sleep . . . I leave from the house, I no gonna say nothing to my wife. But I don't even want a kiss goodbye because maybe I come out, maybe I no go back. That's where I am. I gotta just swallow. . . . Forget about it. Forget about it.

PICCOLO: These people here, they got one fucking idea. They gonna take over. They gonna be the boss . . .

STANFA: Yeah.

PICCOLO: And get rid of us.

STANFA: Yeah. That's what they doing. That's what they done.

The stalking or ''hunting'' of Joey Merlino and his associates began in late June. Day and night Colletti, Brunetti, Battaglia, and Keller cruised the streets of South Philadelphia looking for someone to kill. Merlino, of course, topped the list. The other primary targets were Michael Ciancaglini and Gaeton Lucibello, the guy whose tongue Stanfa wanted to cut out.

Also on the hit list were Michael Avicolli, Stevie

Mazzone, Marty Angelina, Gaetano Scafidi and George Borgesi, all identified as part of the Merlino faction. Eventually, the feds would charge, Stanfa ordered more than a dozen mobsters killed, adding names and targets as his anger, frustration, and paranoia grew.

The feds, watching and listening from the basement of the courthouse in Camden, got most of it on tape, including the growing disenchantment of some of the older members with Stanfa's leadership and Sparacio's startling suggestion that Stanfa step down.

Unlike some of the others, Sparacio had counseled against violence and had urged Stanfa not to go to war with the Merlino faction. Stanfa, who thought Sparacio lacked guts and a backbone, paid little attention to the older mobster who accurately predicted that, "You don't have the right nucleus to put the thing to guns. What do you do? You go out and challenge somebody? We all lose if we don't do it right. . . . We all lose."

At about the same time the feds were shocked to hear Sparacio privately tell Avena that he thought the best course of action was for Stanfa to give up his role as boss and turn over control of the organization to Merlino and his group.

"He don't have the strength to control it," Sparacio said. "Made too many mistakes from the beginning."

"Well, who then is it?" Avena asked. "These young guys?"

"At least, if they got in there, you know where you stand," said Sparacio. "You make a pact. You go along with the program. Let's face it, comes a time, you gotta step aside. He didn't handle the situation from the beginning. All wrong. All wrong. And he can't rectify it.

"Course, I ain't gonna tell him that," Sparacio quickly added.

It wouldn't have mattered.

Stanfa had already decided that the only way to solve the problem, indeed the only way for him to survive, was for Merlino and Mike Ciancaglini to die.

"What it comes down to here," he said, "is they fuck me or I fuck them. That's where we are. . . . What I want to do, I have to take these two guys' head. . . . Then, whatever happens, happens."

But for a while, nothing happened.

It was the La Veranda hit all over again. The San Marco kidnapping in spades. Colletti, Brunetti, Battaglia, and Keller would set up an ambush outside Merlino's apartment, but the young mobster wouldn't show up. Once Colletti had a rifle with a scope and was parked on a highway ramp overlooking Merlino's door. He sat there for half an hour but Skinny Joey was a no-show. On another occasion, he and other crew members were stationed outside a Delaware Avenue nightclub frequented by Merlino and his associates.

"But there were too many people and I didn't want to take a chance on hitting some innocent person," said the repentant hit man after he became a government witness.

On at least a half dozen other occasions, Colletti said, they planted a bomb under or near Merlino's car. It was a staggering tale of underworld incompetence that had jurors rolling their eyes in disbelief.

Colletti said he built the bomb with materials supplied by Brunetti, Battaglia, and Keller. They called it "the egg." It was an eight-inch pipe stuffed with four pounds of black powder explosive and then rigged to a remote control detonation device.

First, Colletti said, Brunetti supplied one of those remote-control packs that kids use for their toy cars. Later they went to a Radio Shack and got a more sophisticated piece of equipment.

It didn't matter.

Every time they set up the bomb, it failed to explode.

"I pushed the button. Sal [Brunetti] pushed the button. Herbie [Keller] pushed the button. Sergio [Battaglia] pushed the button," Colletti said from the witness stand.

The bomb never went off.

"And it's a good thing," Brenda Colletti said later. "When they were having all this trouble, Phil and Sal tested a smaller device at our house. It worked fine and you shoulda heard the explosion."

There are railroad tracks running through a small clump of woods near the home where the Collettis lived in Glassboro. One afternoon, Brenda Colletti said, Phil and Sal came home with a new remote control device, rigged it to a small pipe packed with a spoonful of the black powder and set it up in the woods.

They walked back across the street to Colletti's house and pushed the button.

The explosion reverberated through the neighborhood.

"The cops came. You wouldn't believe the noise," Brenda Colletti said. "We watched from the house."

But in South Philadelphia the bomb was a dud.

Once, Colletti testified, he and Brunetti hid it under some trash along a low brick wall in front of Merlino's car which was parked in his apartment's parking lot. Watching from an abandoned warehouse nearby, Colletti said he and Brunetti saw Merlino come out of his apartment and then pause by the wall.

"He stopped and did some, like, stretching exercises," Colletti said. "He was leaning on the wall right over the trash (and the bomb)."

Colletti pushed the remote control detonation device. Nothing.

He pushed again.

Nothing.

Merlino got in his car and drove away.

On another occasion, Merlino and three of his top associates got into the car without noticing the cardboard box containing the pipe bomb that Colletti had hidden underneath it. As they backed out, Colletti pushed the switch. Nothing. Then as he and Battaglia watched, the car drove away, dragging the box for several hundred feet before it broke free.

The would-be hit men scurried into the street and scooped it up; Merlino and his associates remained unaware of how close they had come to being launched.

In between attempts, Colletti kept the bomb in his house in Glassboro, storing it in the bedroom closet or in one of the kitchen cupboards. "They assured me it wasn't dangerous," Brenda Colletti said. "They said it wouldn't go off or I woulda never let them put it in my house."

During the mob war, the Collettis also stored pistols, machine guns, and silencers in their basement. "Phil was good at fixin' things and they would bring stuff over, guns and silencers, for him to work on," Brenda explained. "He had all his plumbing tools. Then they would test fire them down in the basement."

Brenda Colletti, listening as she cooked or made coffee, eventually became a part of the plotting that took place around her kitchen table. After weeks of trying and failing to get Merlino, Brunetti came up with the idea of using her "charms" to pull off a hit.

"He said he could get some cyanide," Brenda Colletti said. "And he said I could get dressed up in something sexy, a slinky dress, ya know, and go to one of these clubs on Delaware Avenue where Merlino and his friends were and slip the poison into their drinks."

Brenda Colletti said she considered the idea.

"It got crazy," she said. "You got to a point where you were hearing this every day and it was like, it's kill or be killed. Philip used to go out every night and I would pray he didn't come home with any holes in him. So, yeah, I guess I woulda done it. At the time I think I woulda. But Philip said no way. He didn't want me to get involved."

Later that was not an option, but at first Philip Colletti kept his wife at a distance. She knew what was going on. She heard the discussions, even took part in some of them. But he didn't want her to be a part of anything. He didn't want her to be a player.

It went on like that for most of June and July 1993. No hits. Many misses. Stanfa became more and more frustrated. He wanted some action. He wanted somebody dead. He was tired of the excuses and explanations. He was, in fact, a lot like Nicky Scarfo.

Stanfa might have talked about honor and loyalty and respect, but he was really interested in only one thing: money. He said as much in a conversation with Tommy Gambino, whose father and uncle were convicted New York-based Sicilian heroin dealers.

"You know, there's these . . . Americans," Stanfa

said to Gambino, "and what they want to do at this juncture is to throw me out so they can . . . because there's a sea of opportunities here. You know what I mean? A river of money can be made, in all respects, but as I'm telling you, you know, what's needed is a little push."

Eventually, Stanfa decided to look to New York and Sicily for help in arranging that little push. It was then that he asked Gambino to inquire about the possibility of recruiting "unknown faces," gunmen who were strangers to the Merlino faction. In two conversations with Gambino, Stanfa laid his problems on the line, complaining about Merlino's luck and his own misfortune and toying with the idea of going to Sicily himself to seek help.

The conversations, in Sicilian, were later translated by Steve Salvo, the FBI language expert assigned to the case. Salvo, like Stanfa, had been born in Sicily and spoke the dialect fluently.

FBI Surveillance Tape
June 18, 1993
10:43 A.M.

JOHN STANFA: See, how it is, now, these guys are a
　　bunch of louses who deserve to have their heads taken
　　off. As a matter of fact, we're working on this. Since
　　over here, what do you think, I do not have capable
　　people here. God damn. There's no one. There's no
　　one. I do not even have . . .
TOMASO GAMBINO: Like I said, we're here at your dis-
　　posal. Whatever you need . . . John, I want you to
　　know this. Because we have always been . . . you and
　　my father.
STANFA: I know. Tommy, now what I want to say to you,

what I need here is some . . . unknown faces because these cuckolds know everyone. If they're Italian, no one knows them.

(Later)

STANFA: They are causing me lots of problems. They're truly, to tell you the truth, they're driving me crazy. Now we've reached a point that they either fuck me or I fuck them. . . . Now this is the situation. If you can commit to giving me a helping hand . . . you know, have a young man . . . we have everything. The only thing that's needed are four unknown faces . . . these guys, because right now they are being cautious. Fuck. They walk and they walk like this.

GAMBINO: Okay. Yeah.

STANFA: As soon as possible. Then if you tell me when, we'll meet . . .

GAMBINO: Fuck. If we do not help each other, then . . .

STANFA: Tommy, I'm here at your disposal. I feel bad because I need help. Because see how it is, I am alone. What do I mean by this. I do not have anybody of our own blood.

GAMBINO: Okay. Now I'm going down there. Let's see what we can do and I'll come back down.

STANFA: Beautiful.

GAMBINO: Make contact and we'll do what we have to do.

STANFA: Beautiful. Beautiful. To tell you the truth, this is something important because without a hit man . . .

GAMBINO: Sure. After a cleanup you'll feel better.

STANFA: Sure. It has to be done. And then in any case here we can. . . . You know what I mean?

GAMBINO: As long as we help each other regarding this matter.

June 22, 1993
12:42 P.M.

STANFA: Now this is what I want to do . . . if God grants me the grace for this situation . . . if worse comes to

worse, fuck, I'll get on a plane and go to Italy and I'll
go there . . .

GAMBINO: Yeah. That's what I was thinking.

STANFA: . . . and I'll tell them the situation. Now, if I go
there . . . since too much publicity has been created
here, if the cops know that I'm in contact with . . .
your family. . . . And I didn't want to do this because,
I said to myself, when they see me go there, it's not.
. . . Over there, all the doors are opened to us. . . .
Over there, regarding this we do not have any problems over there.

GAMBINO: Because here . . . you cannot stay, you have
to do something.

STANFA: Yes. . . . What I want to do, you know, I have
to shoot these two guys. Not even if . . . and then
whatever happens, happens.

(*Later*)

STANFA: As I told you, they're cuckolds. They're cuckolds. There's this Joe Merlino. Merlino motherfucker.

(*Later*)

STANFA: God damn, I'm all alone. It seems that God is
picking on me, you know what I mean? I have to over-
see everything. And I do not want in the future that a
mistake. . . . It's no one else. It's me. . . . If it goes
well, it's me. If it goes bad, it's me. I'm like an object
falling out of the sky with the earth below catching
me.

GAMBINO: I know . . .

STANFA: See, the last time, time I went over . . . God
damn, five cars were following me . . . without saying
anything to anyone about going here, there. Change
car and thing, nothing. Five cars followed me . . . because, justifiably, even if you purchase a ticket . . .

GAMBINO: They know it!

STANFA: They know you and they. . . . Now when I do
this, fuck, a bomb as such shows up. What will people
think? That I went to seek help over there. And already . . . I'm hot. I did not want to heat it up more
than what it is.

GAMBINO: I know, but John . . . if you get this chance to go over there . . . my opinion is that it's a good thing because we, this, we have this type of mentality. We're the same.

STANFA: Yeah . . . the only thing needed is a stroke of luck. Do you know what he [Merlino] does; every night he goes out. . . . Now he goes out and he goes to Wildwood. He goes to restaurants. He goes here and he goes there. And he always has three, four guys around him.

GAMBINO: He always has three or four?

STANFA: Yeah. Sometime more. Sometime less. . . . Now the way things are set up, then if God is going to punish me, you know, the way things are set up, it should be all right. Because he has, he lives in an apartment . . . and parks the car.

GAMBINO: It would be good.

Eventually, Stanfa got word back from Gambino that no help was available. The mobsters in New York and Sicily who might be able to assist him had too many problems of their own. There was the heat of ongoing investigations and the plague of informants. Sammy Gravano was testifying against John Gotti in New York and the Gambino family there was in a shambles. In Sicily, the brutal murders of anti-Mafia magistrates Giovanni Falcone and Paolo Borsellino a year earlier had unleashed an unprecedented crackdown that included widespread public support for the government in its push to find and prosecute the killers of the two highly regarded judges. Even high-ranking Catholic Church leaders in Italy were speaking out against the Mafia.

On both sides of the Atlantic, then, La Cosa Nostra was under siege.

At about this time, Frank Martines recruited a new shooter for the Stanfa organization.

He was not one of the "unknown faces" Stanfa said he needed, but he fit the bill in other ways. Hard as nails, coldly efficient and seemingly without any morals, John Veasey had the ability to make things happen.

He proved to be a deadly accurate hit man.

First for the mob.

Then for the feds.

10

Junkie, armed robber, hustler, wife-beater, and bully, "John John" Veasey was the complete package, the ultimate lowlife mobster. He had a rap sheet that ran on for nearly a dozen pages and, at twenty-nine, had spent nearly half his adult life behind bars.

He had finished his last stint—for drugs, assault, and robbery—on March 10, 1993, eight days after the Joey Ciancaglini hit that sent the Stanfa organization careening out of control.

At the time, none of that meant anything to Veasey. He wasn't a wiseguy, nor did he pretend to be. He knew some people who were connected—growing up in South Philadelphia it was almost impossible not to know somebody who knew somebody—but the power struggle between Stanfa and Skinny Joey Merlino wasn't anything he cared about.

Veasey told anyone who would listen that he wanted to get his life in order, a claim that raised skepticism in certain quarters where his reputation as a headbanger and a drug addict was well established.

"He was scum," says a local wiseguy.

Veasey never knew his father. His mother had had a drug problem for much of her life. He had dropped out of school in the sixth grade and had been an intravenous drug user—coke, heroin, meth—from the age of thirteen. He had been arrested dozens of times for robbery, assault, and drug use, but later said that the only time he killed was after he had been recruited by Martines to join the Stanfa mob. He considered himself a hit man-for-hire.

"I robbed to support a drug habit," he explained. "I murdered for money. It's two different things."

He claimed that he had stopped using drugs cold turkey while in jail—"September 27, 1991 . . . State Correctional Institute of Frackville," he would say—and that he had promised his older brother, Billy, and several other members of his family that this time it was for good. But it would be a while longer before he kicked his penchant for violence. And in the summer of 1993 that made him an attractive recruit for the Stanfa mob.

Later a federal prosecutor would ask him what his method was for resolving disputes during the days when he terrorized the streets of South Philadelphia.

"My method is to fight or to . . . you know, that's the way I handled things," Veasey said.

Hard, tough, and a little bit crazy, that's what they said about John John Veasey—and willing to do almost anything for money.

Fresh out of prison, Veasey moved back in with his common-law wife in a rowhouse near Seventh Street and Washington Avenue. There were, at different times, six different children living in the house—some hers, some his, some theirs. Their relationship, Veasey conceded, was marred by domestic violence and drug abuse.

"My wife, she musta had me arrested fifteen, twenty times," he said. "Sometimes she'd do it just to steal my drugs."

Veasey once brutally beat a man who died later that night, but he said the death was the result of a drug overdose. Again, it was a domestic situation.

"My wife's ex-husband," Veasey said. "His wife and my wife, they were also fighting. It was, like, a family thing. . . . I beat him up pretty bad and they tried to blame me for killing him. [But] he drove away in his car. He died in a hotel hours later of an overdose."

When he was released from prison in 1993, Veasey went to work as a laborer for a construction company, collecting his wages off the books until his parole officer complained—something about wanting to see a pay stub and proof of gainful employment, about playing by the rules, about not slipping up and falling back into that old routine.

Parole had become a big part of Veasey's life and he didn't want to screw it up. Because of his extensive arrest record and long history of drug abuse, he had to report to his parole officer once a week and submit to urine tests virtually on demand. He would later brag about how, through all the strife and aggravation that followed, he never failed a drug test, never gave a dirty urine sample. It was a strange value system. He would willingly murder, maim, and extort for the mob. But at the same time, he would report to his parole officer each week. In fact, he once called off a planned ambush in order to make a parole appointment. And he would pee in a cup on command and boast about how his urine always tested drug free.

By the summer of 1993, Veasey was mixing cement for a concrete company owned by John Stanfa's brother-in-law. The work made him even harder, broadening his chest and bulking up the muscles in his arms and neck which already bulged from months of lifting weights in prison.

Veasey stood just five-foot-six. But he weighed a rock-solid 200 pounds. He was part of a construction crew working at the Philadelphia College of Pharmacy and Science. Martines, Stanfa's acting underboss, had a tile-setting business and was also on the job. Martines made it a point to meet Veasey. During one conversation, Veasey said, Martines asked him if he knew Joey Merlino.

Veasey said he did.

Then, he said, Martines cocked his finger and thumb into the shape of a gun and asked Veasey if he'd be willing to go after Merlino.

Veasey said he would.

And that, Veasey told a federal jury, was how he became a hit man for the mob. That same afternoon, Veasey said, Martines drove him over to the Continental Food warehouse, which was just a few blocks from the construction site, and introduced him to the crime boss.

"This is the new kid I told ya about," Martines said to Stanfa.

Veasey stood awkwardly off to the side after the introduction, picking up bits and pieces of the conversation between the bald, barrel-chested mob boss and the equally stocky, dark-haired Martines. He heard that Martines planned to put him with "Phil and Sal" and saw that Stanfa agreed with that.

"Good luck," Stanfa told him when the conversation ended.

This, by Veasey's account, was toward the end of July. For more than a month, Phil Colletti, Sal Brunetti, Sergio Battaglia, and Herb Keller had been stalking Merlino without success.

Stanfa, frustrated and angry, wanted something done. He had lost patience. His frustration was obvious in a rambling conversation he had with Tommy Gambino in Avena's office on July 23, about a week before Veasey was brought on the scene.

As in the other conversations with Gambino, Stanfa spoke in Sicilian and the difference was clearly reflected in the way he turned a phrase. There was none of the hemming and hawing that marked his conversations in English, none of the fractured or disjointed sentences, no struggle to find the right words. Clear and concise, Stanfa laid it all out.

"We've played every card," Stanfa said. "We know all their movements. Everything. The situation is such that on three, four occasions we've come close . . . and, eh, for one reason or another, but, as I've told you, we're continuing. . . . We have everything. We're equipped with everything."

As he spoke, it became clear to the FBI agents that Stanfa wasn't just talking about Merlino. He had long range plans to clean house, to resolve all his problems, and to solidify his hold on the organization. Merlino and Mike Ciancaglini would be the first to go, but down the road there would also be a reception for Ralph Natale, the veteran mobster who was backing Merlino from prison.

"He's due to come out in sixteen, seventeen months,"

Stanfa said, "and as soon as he comes out, to tell you the truth, he has to die . . . if it's not the first day, second day, first week that he comes out. I don't even want to give him time to breathe the air because of what this cuckold is doing. I haven't done anything to him. This slime . . . he's nobody."

From there Stanfa went on to berate Merlino and those around him.

He called the young mobster a "degenerate . . . a worthless person . . . truly a drunkard . . . a true nothingness . . . a prick." Gambino said little, occasionally uttering words of agreement.

It was all Stanfa, a Sicilian soliloquy—part King Lear and part Don Corleone. He complained of a "hex" put on him by Biagio Adornetto, the missing mobster. He worried about "the evil eye." He planned and plotted.

They can't even shine our shoes, Tommy. That's the situation. And . . . it's useless. There's a saying that states when a fish starts to smell, it starts from the head. The head has to be cut, otherwise it will smell. . . . I'll kill him. . . . Let's kill him.

The groups here are total trash, you know what I mean Tommy? . . . He has trash following him. . . . Tommy, in a few words, these people are, there's quantity, not quality. To us, as I stated earlier, they can't even shine our shoes because, at least, we know where we come from. We know that it's honorable to have this because . . . in our neck of the woods we say, "First comes honor and respect. Without these requisites you're not a man." Instead, these people are competing in the cuckold contest. They marry someone who is married. With this one and that one. The wife . . . fuck, he's in one place and the wife, fuck, eh, that's the way it is. Because there's proof. It's not like I'm saying this because I don't like them. No. There's proof. . . .

No, you know what's needed here? Renovation. You know, you have to try to do a demolition.

Less than two weeks later, on August 5, 1993, the renovation work began.

It happened almost by accident.

Colletti and Veasey had been on an assignment earlier that morning, a plot to murder Merlino associate Steve Mazzone. They had set up an ambush in a park near the Continental Food warehouse. Mazzone had been spotted there a few days before, apparently stalking Stanfa. The plan was to lay a trap and gun him down. But Mazzone hadn't shown up that morning and the hit was called off.

A few hours later, almost on a lark, Colletti decided to drive by Sixth and Catharine Streets in South Philadelphia, where the Merlino crew had recently moved into a new clubhouse.

"Let's scope it out," he told Veasey.

Now, a little after one o'clock in the afternoon, Colletti and Veasey were sitting in a car watching a low-slung, modern brick building that had once been the local headquarters for Greenpeace, the environmental group. A Greenpeace sign still hung over the door.

The FBI also had the joint in focus.

A surveillance camera was trained on the front door, but the feds had not yet gotten around to bugging the building. The camera was mounted on a pole across the street, similar to the surveillance setup at the Warfield when Joey Chang got hit.

It was a bright, sunny Thursday afternoon, the kind of day made for Italian water ice and a game of half ball. Heat was rising off the concrete sidewalks in waves. Anyone with the chance to go was already talking about a weekend at the shore.

John Veasey and Phil Colletti had other things on their minds, however.

Colletti, sitting in the front seat of a white Ford Taurus and looking through a pair of binoculars, spotted Merlino and Ciancaglini. The two mobsters walked out of the clubhouse, stopped to talk with several other guys who were hanging on the corner in front of the building, and then proceeded alone up Catharine Street, away from where Colletti and Veasey were parked.

Colletti started the engine and the Ford Taurus inched its way up the block. Now it was even with the clubhouse. Then John Veasey noticed that his brother Billy was one of the guys standing on the corner and he called Colletti off.

"Phil, we can't go. My brother will see me," Veasey said.

Frustrated, Colletti circled the block and took up his surveillance position again. By the time they were back in place, Billy Veasey had left the corner. And there, strolling on the sidewalk heading back down toward the clubhouse, were Merlino and Ciancaglini. Both seemed to be enjoying the sun and warmth of the August afternoon. Neither seemed to have a care in the world.

Colletti told Veasey to get in the back of the car. Veasey rolled the rear passenger side window open. Colletti rolled down the front passenger side window and drove slowly up the block. The car passed through the FBI surveillance shot, from right to left. Like the Warfield ambush on Joe Ciancaglini, the action in this hit would take place off camera. Colletti held the steering wheel with one hand. In the other he had a .45 caliber semiautomatic. Veasey, in the back seat, had a 9mm that Sal Brunetti had given him that morning. As the car came abreast of Merlino and Ciancaglini, Colletti and Veasey opened fire.

The sidewalk erupted. Merlino, hit once in the buttocks, spun and went down. Ciancaglini threw up his left arm in a fruitless attempt to ward off the gunfire. A bullet ripped through his bicep and tore into his chest. The impact spun him around. He fell, got up and then fell down again with a thud.

Colletti and Veasey emptied their pistols, firing wildly in the direction of the two bodies. Then Colletti gunned the engine and the Ford Taurus disappeared into the warren of crissing-crossing streets in that tightly constructed section of South Philadelphia.

The mob war that the FBI had been hearing about for months was now out in the open. The gunfire that rang out that afternoon would soon echo through South Philadelphia.

Like the ambush at the Warfield, police were on the scene within minutes, questioning residents, passersby, and the guys on the corner. Mike Ciancaglini and Merlino were rushed to the hospital. Ciancaglini was DOA. Merlino was admitted with a bullet in the buttocks, a wound that was more painful than life-threatening.

The hit was carried out with precision. The only flaw was that Merlino survived.

But the aftermath was another story.

Within hours, Colletti was a prime suspect. Within days, so was Veasey.

Where to begin?

It has long been a fundamental rule in the underworld that you don't use a gun that can be traced back to you when you carry out a hit. Likewise, you don't use a vehicle that would link you to the crime.

The white Ford Taurus that Colletti drove that afternoon was leased *in his own name* from a car dealership owned by Sergio Battaglia's family in Hammonton, New Jersey. When police found the car abandoned and on fire three hours after the shooting, they immediately ran a trace. The car matched the description of the vehicle used in the ambush of Ciancaglini and Merlino. When it came back leased in the name of one known Stanfa associate and owned by a company tied to another, detectives knew they were onto something.

There was more.

After the shooting, Colletti and Veasey drove to an old garage near Juniper Street in South Philadelphia that the Stanfa organization used to store weapons. They cleaned up and left their guns, which were later dumped in acid before being thrown into the Absecon Inlet near Atlantic City. That, at least, was standard post-hit procedure in the underworld.

From there the two hit men drove to the home of Colletti's parents, a rowhouse near 18th and McKean Streets, and planned what to do next. After trying without success for more than an hour to reach Battaglia and Keller on the phone, Colletti called his wife, Brenda, and told her to drive over to South Philadelphia. She would later call the police and fabricate a story about the Taurus having been stolen earlier that morning.

But first she helped her husband and Veasey torch the car.

Veasey got a plastic gallon container of milk out of the refrigerator, dumped what was left of the milk into the sink, borrowed a dollar from Colletti—"I was broke. I didn't have no money"—and walked down the block to a gas station where he bought a gallon of gas.

"Then we proceeeded to go burn the car," he said.

They drove to an isolated area near an old bus barn a dozen blocks from the Colletti rowhouse. Veasey said he knew the area well, and had abandoned stolen cars there before. Brenda Colletti, who had followed in her car, watched as Veasey poured gasoline in and around the white Ford Taurus and her husband removed anything from the vehicle that might be used as evidence.

"Phil was cleaning stuff out of the car and I was pouring gas all over the car, you know, making sure the windows were a little down . . . so it would, you know, burn," Veasey recalled. "I poured gas all around the doors, all . . . around the tires, all in the trunk.

"And then I was, I seen some change in there from going back and forth over the bridge with Phil."

So John Veasey, the hit man who didn't have any money, reached into the car for the coins.

"I wanted to get the change out," he said. "When I went to get the change, (Phil) threw the match in the car and the car went up . . . and so did my hand."

Veasey's left hand, soaked in gasoline, ignited as the car burst into flames. Veasey tried to roll his hand up in the front of his shirt, to smother the fire. But he had spilled gasoline on his shirt and the fire just burned stronger. Next he tried to pat his burning hand out on the front of his pants, but they also were soaked in gasoline.

"It was like saturated," Veasey said. "It wouldn't go out. It just burned."

Finally, with Colletti's help, he was able to smother the flames and put out the fire. Colletti then helped him into his wife's car and they drove back to the rowhouse.

Veasey, the skin on his hand already blistered and peeling off, wanted to go to a hospital. But Colletti cautioned against it. That would only attract more attention. Instead, they packed Veasey's hand in ice cubes and plotted an alibi.

In a few hours, it was decided, Brenda Colletti would call the police. She would tell them she had spent the night at her in-laws' home and that when she went to look for her car late in the afternoon, it was gone. Philip, she would say, had been at their home in Glassboro all day.

Veasey's alibi was that he was on the construction site. Stanfa had arranged for him to be clocked in and out of the job. Now, a little after three in the afternoon, it was time for Veasey to go home.

Phil Colletti, who was driving back to Glassboro, dropped Veasey within a block of his house near Seventh and Washington Streets. Veasey, his hand throbbing, gingerly got out of the car, ripped off a makeshift bandage and stuck his badly burned hand in his pants pocket. Then he walked up the street where he lived, making sure that several neighbors saw him.

"My mother-in-law and sister-in-law was sitting outside, so I asked her for a cigarette,'' Veasey said. "So she'd see that I came home from work . . . in case anybody asked any questions.''

Veasey took the cigarette and went into his house.

Over the years Veasey had built up a reputation for being both tough and crazy. Fearless in a fight, he could take a punch as well as give one. Completely without scruples, he would use whatever was at hand to pummel an opponent into the ground.

Now he turned that same mindset on himself.

Even the feds, hearing the story for the first time, cringed when he told them what happened next.

It was a simple, logical extension of events. His hand was badly burned. So was the car used in a mob murder. How to distance himself from the event and yet be able to explain the blackened and blistered mass on the end of his left arm?

He had left the job site uninjured. Workers there, at Stanfa's urging, would tell that to anyone who asked. And now he had his mother-in-law and some other neighbors ready to say they saw nothing unusual when he got home that night.

Three hours after murdering Mike Ciancaglini and an hour after accidentally setting his hand on fire, John Veasey walked into the tiny backyard of his South Philadelphia rowhouse and reached for a can of lighter fluid that was next to a small barbecue grill.

It is not hard to imagine beads of sweat forming on his broad forehead and rivulets trickling down his back as he prepared for what he was about to do. It is one thing to accidentally set your hand on fire. It is something else again to do it intentionally.

Veasey took a deep breath and poured the flammable liquid on his already burned and blistered left hand. Then he struck a match and set it on fire again.

"I started screaming," Veasey said, "so the neighbors come out and I have witnesses that I burned my hand, you know . . . That's what I told the hospital, too. I said I burned it on a grill. You know, the new gas grills. I told them I put lighter fluid in and I didn't know you got to push the button, and then it blew up on me."

Brenda Colletti was questioned by police for three hours that night after reporting her car stolen. She knew as soon as detectives from the homicide unit arrived for her debriefing that the cops weren't buying her story, but she stuck to it.

Two weeks later, she and Philip were subpoenaed before a federal grand jury conducting "an organized crime homicide investigation." On the advice of their lawyer, Salvatore J. Avena, the Collettis both exercised their Fourth, Fifth and Fourteenth Amendment rights and refused to answer any questions.

Veasey's story about the barbecue grill also failed to impress the FBI or the Philadelphia Police Department's organized crime unit. Both tabbed him as the second suspect in the Merlino-Ciancaglini shooting within days.

On August 10, 1993, Michael Ciancaglini was buried following a funeral mass at the Epiphany of Our Lord Roman Catholic Church near Twelfth and Wolf Streets in the heart of South Philadelphia. The church was not far from the corner where Ciancaglini, Merlino, and a handful of the other young mobsters had hung out while growing up as kids. Hundreds of people, including most of those tied to the Merlino faction of the mob, turned out for the service.

Merlino, grim-faced and walking with a cane, had little to say when a television reporter approached him outside the funeral parlor prior to the mass. Smoking a cigarette as he waited for the funeral entourage to leave for the church, Merlino was asked if he had any comment about the events of the past five days.

"Go fuck yourself," the young mob leader said.

At the time, most of the pundits in law enforcement and the media were predicting the Merlino crew would soon crumble. Mike Ciancaglini was carried out of church in a box that morning. Joey Merlino left leaning on a cane. And that, the savvy commentators said, summed up the status of the renegade faction. "It's just a matter of time," said one investigator. "Joey's a walking dead man."

But not everyone was convinced there would be a quick and easy end to the hostilities.

"I wouldn't be surprised if that thin guy starts to act up again," Avena told Sparacio in a conversation the FBI bug picked up about a week after the funeral.

"I wouldn't doubt it," said the ever-practical Sparacio. "That's why, you know, you don't make heads or tails of what you can do and what you can't do yet. . . . Start out doing something, you got to finish it. Anymore, everything's just shoddy."

Three days later, Avena and Piccolo also discussed the turmoil in a conversation that focused primarily on loyalty—or the lack of it—within Philadelphia's Cosa Nostra. Both had been surprised to learn that Salvatore "Wayne" Grande, a convicted mob soldier from the

Scarfo crime family, was now cooperating with authorities from prison.

Grande was serving a thirty-eight-year federal sentence following his conviction with Scarfo and fifteen
others on racketeering charges in 1988. His brother Joe,
another mob soldier, was doing forty years. They were
the sons of John "Coo Coo" Grande, an old Bruno family soldier who had recently died.

While Wayne Grande could not have any impact on
the Stanfa organization, his decision to turn was yet another embarrassment for the Philadelphia mob. What's
more, it brought shame to his family. In fact, Piccolo
pointed out, the Grandes had been so embarrassed by
Wayne Grande's decision to flip that they didn't even
mention his name in the obituary when John Grande
died.

FBI Surveillance Tape
August 23, 1993
4:36 P.M.

SALVATORE AVENA: How about . . . what's his . . . is he,
   he turned the other way, right? That Wayne?
ANTHONY PICCOLO: Oh yeah.
AVENA: But is he making out any cases against anybody?
PICCOLO: Tell you the truth, Sal, I haven't heard anything. Nothing whatsoever. Now, has he done anything? Locally, no. I haven't heard anything, of
   course.
AVENA: Well, where could he go if it's not local?
PICCOLO: There's nobody left. I mean, you know, locally.
   Ah, as far as his wife is concerned, she's divorcing
   him. His father disowned him. Even when he died, he
   wasn't mentioned in the obituary. The old man was so
   embarrassed, Sal. I'll tell you one thing, he was a
   classy. . . . He went around and told everybody that

his son had turned and so forth and so on.

AVENA: What's he gain by that, though? They reducing his sentence or what are they doing?

PICCOLO: I don't know, don't know, Sal. Are they using him for different things? Who the hell knows. I don't know. But he'll call the kids once in a while. He has a boy and a girl.

AVENA: And he does call the kids?

PICCOLO: He calls them once a while, but who the hell knows where he's at. His wife doesn't speak to him or talk to him at all.

AVENA: What a cross to carry for the rest of their lives. Number one, the kids gotta feel that my father was dishonorable.

PICCOLO: Certainly. Sure.

AVENA: Number two, they lost a father to begin with.

PICCOLO: They lost a father.

AVENA: They lost a father. They gotta suffer with the . . . the humility.

PICCOLO: Sure, the stigma that stays with them. It's a shame, two nice kids.

Later in the same conversation, the FBI heard Avena and Piccolo talking about the problems with the Merlino faction. Again, loyalty and honor were the issues. If anything, Piccolo said, Stanfa had started out being too liberal with the young mobsters. In turn, he said, the young mobsters had taken advantage, interpreting his liberal attitude as a sign of weakness.

AVENA: What was the inducement for so many to go to the other side? Where's the inducement? I mean, obviously people don't . . . believe in tradition then.

PICCOLO: Well, no question. No question about that, Sal. . . . The only thing, and I've tried to analyze it more, that maybe they have a feeling that this fella would be too stern.

AVENA: No harm in that.

PICCOLO: That's exactly right, and yet, he didn't show that. He's been very liberal with them, you know, at the very beginning Sal. But to me, from the remarks that were passed, like, you know, "greaseball" and "dago guinea" and all that amongst them and the word, you know, goes back. Which he's aware of, you know. But that's the kind of attitude that they had. So I don't know. . . . But in other words, everything was fair game, Sal. Whichever way they wanted to go, that's the way they went. Beating people up. Shaking people down. . . . They really got carried away, Sal.

With Mike Ciancaglini dead and Merlino wounded, Stanfa appeared to be in the driver's seat. Clearly, he thought he was. Three weeks after Mike Ciancaglini was killed, he was heard discussing with Battaglia plans to take over the extortion rackets that the Merlino faction had been running.

"I no gonna go to the people and. . . . twist their arm," he said. "I wanna do nice, nice way. . . . But in the meantime, they gotta understand, this thing is one."

No more factions. No more disorganized shakedowns. Now everyone would be paying the same organization.

"They get scared, they give the money, you understand," Stanfa said.

He also mentioned that he had a few more scores to settle. Stanfa would not be a gracious victor in the mob war. Skittish and paranoid when he was the target, he now became arrogant and vindictive. Among other things, he took aim at Joseph Santaguida, a prominent criminal attorney in Philadelphia who had represented Gary Tavella in the kidnapping case, but who also was Merlino's lawyer.

Stanfa didn't like Santaguida's attitude. He thought

the lawyer hadn't shown him or those around him the proper respect. And so he planned to kill him.

"I got Santaguida over here," Stanfa told Avena and Piccolo, apparently meaning he was putting the matter on hold but would eventually deal with it. "Who he think he is? I gonna cripple him. I gotta be honest with you. Right now I got my own thing, but he gonna be next."

In fact, it was Stanfa and his son, Joe, who were next.

11

John Stanfa's arrogant posturing didn't last long.

A week after he boasted to Piccolo and Avena about his plans for the future, he was ducking for cover in the midst of rush hour traffic on one of the busiest highways in the city.

More reminiscent of Sicily than South Philadelphia, the attempt on Stanfa's life took the escalating mob war to a new and more brutal level. Now everyone was fair game.

Stanfa had moved with his family to a sprawling ranch-style home in Medford, New Jersey, early in 1993. He still owned a rowhouse on Passyunk Avenue in South Philadelphia, but the house in Medford, which sat on nearly five acres and was in a semi-rural area, provided better living accomodations and, more important, better security.

The home, valued at about $280,000, was listed in the names of his son, Joe, and daughter, Sara. There was a horseshoe-shaped driveway out front and a barbecue pit and bocce ball court in the back. Stanfa hosted a big July Fourth party that summer for most of the members of the organization, and frequently conducted business in the basement or recreation room. The nearest neighbors were several hundred yards away, giving the mob boss the kind of privacy that was impossible to find in South Philadelphia.

Stanfa and his son Joe commuted from Medford each morning to the Continental Imported Foods warehouse in the Grays Ferry section of South Philadelphia. It was about a forty-five minute trip, depending on traffic, and, in a move steeped in both arrogance and stupidity, Stanfa seldom varied his route.

The Stanfas left the house at the same time each morning, traveled the same highways, drove in the same car. Only the drivers changed. Alternately, Ron Previte, an ex-Philadelphia cop, and Freddy Aldrich, a Vietnam War veteran, were behind the wheel.

Previte, who became a soldier in the Stanfa crime family despite his previous employment as a law enforcement officer, Aldrich, a decorated Marine Corps veteran, and Vince Filipelli, a hulking weightlifter and former Mister America, made up what the cops called Stanfa's "palace guard" at the time. One of the three was always at the mob boss's side.

On the morning of August 31, 1993, Aldrich was driving the slightly beat-up and unremarkable 1976 silver-gray Cadillac Seville that ferried Stanfa and his son to work. Later police would credit the burly vet with saving the lives of the mob boss and his son. Still later others would argue that if Stanfa had not been so bullheaded, so self-assured—that if he had listened to Previte and some others and had changed his daily routine—the ambush could have been avoided.

But Stanfa had always underestimated the kids, the "little Americans." And on this morning he would pay a price for that arrogance, a price extracted in his own son's blood.

At the time, Joe Stanfa was not a member of his father's crime family. The kid, handsome, dark-haired, and with angular features that favored his mother Lena's side of the family, worked long and hard at the food business. According to the cops who had the place under surveillance, he was the mainstay in the warehouse, supervising crews, seeing that orders were filled and delivered on time, and even doing some of the bull work if business started to back up and deliveries were running behind schedule.

John Stanfa, on the other hand, would be up in an office on the second floor conducting business that had little to do with the price of provolone or the availability of prosciutto. Continental became, the feds later charged, a stash house where Stanfa would hide in the walls and ceiling tens of thousands of dollars generated by the mob's illegal gambling and extortion rackets. It was the nerve center and headquarters of the organization.

On any given day, if you wanted to find John Stanfa, Continental was the first place you would look.

The Cadillac Seville traveled west on Route 70 and then south on Interstate 295 toward the Walt Whitman Bridge, joining the flow of thousands of commuters who headed over the Delaware River into Philadelphia each morning. Along the way, an unmarked white 1993 Chevrolet Astro van, which had been stolen about two months earlier, fell in line a few hundred feet behind. Both vehicles passed through the toll booths at the base of the bridge in Philadelphia and then continued west along the Schuylkill Expressway, the maddeningly congested highway that skirts the edge of downtown Philadelphia.

The expressway is a concrete cattle chute during the morning rush, cars careening around the tightly banked curves almost bumper-to-bumper at forty and fifty miles an hour. As Stanfa's Cadillac cruised toward the Vare Avenue/Mifflin Street exit just above Grays Ferry, the white van pulled up along the passenger side. In a flash, curtains were pulled away from two makeshift portholes that had been cut into the side of the vehicle. Now the barrels of two 9mm machine pistols were pointing down at the Seville. Stanfa, in the front passenger seat, ducked as a spray of bullets shattered the window next to his head. Joe, riding in the back seat directly behind his father, was not as quick.

One of the bullets caught him high in the face, cracking his right cheekbone. He slid to the floor in agony. Another bullet ripped through the rear tire. Stanfa screamed for Aldrich to stop, that Joe had been hit. Blood was all over the back seat where Joe Stanfa lay moaning. Instead, Aldrich rammed the side of the van, forcing it onto the Vare Avenue exit ramp, then he gunned the engine of the Caddy and continued west on the expressway for another half mile, exiting at University Avenue.

With smoke and the smell of burning rubber trailing in its wake—the rear passenger-side tire was now in shreds—the Cadillac lurched around the corner at Thirty-fourth and Wharton and pulled up in front of the Warfield Luncheon Express where six months earlier Joey Ciancaglini had been gunned down.

Joe Stanfa was hustled out of the car and into another. He was rushed to the Hospital of the University of Penn-

sylvania about a mile away. There emergency room doctors scrambled to stop the bleeding. Joe was quickly
admitted in critical condition. His status remained touch-
and-go for about forty-eight hours.

Through it all, he was conscious and alert. And
through it all, he told police investigating the shooting
nothing. John Stanfa and Aldrich also stonewalled the
cops, Stanfa deciding to deal with the matter in his own
way and in his own time.

The van was recovered two days later, abandoned on
a neighborhood street about three blocks from the Continental warehouse.

No one has ever been charged with the shooting.

Joe Stanfa spent nearly two weeks in the hospital before being released. Months later he returned for another
emergency operation after a life-threatening blood clot
formed. Today a pockmark about the size of a dime high
on his right cheekbone is testimony to the botched hit.

The scars in the Philadelphia underworld, however,
run much deeper.

In addition to enraging Stanfa, the ambush on the
Schuylkill Expressway galvanized law enforcement. It
was one thing for mob bodies to turn up in shallow
graves along rural roads in South Jersey or bound and
gagged in the trunks of cars abandoned in South Philadelphia. It was another matter for a hit to take place in
the midst of rush-hour traffic on the city's most heavily
traveled highway.

The Philadelphia Police Department and the FBI, already working together and sharing information, decided
to turn up the heat on the wiseguys. It was time, said
one investigator, to ''bust balls.''

"Routine traffic stops" became the norm for any known associates of Stanfa or Merlino seen driving around South Philadelphia. Over the next two months, eight different mobsters were arrested for carrying weapons. The guns, .380, .45 and .38 caliber semiautomatics, were confiscated. Almost every one of those charges was later dropped because of the questionable nature of the stop and search. But that wasn't the point. The idea was to create some havoc in the underworld, to establish a police presence, and to get some of the weapons off the streets.

"It's total fucking insanity," Salvatore Sparacio said just hours after Joe Stanfa was shot.

The feds couldn't have agreed more.

FBI Surveillance Tape
August 31, 1993
11:50 A.M.

SALVATORE AVENA: You know what happened this morning, don't you?

SALVATORE SPARACIO: Yeah, I just heard. Motherfuckers. They ain't gonna stop. . . . See, these things are unprecedented. You never touch family . . . crazy. Total fucking insanity.

AVENA: Isn't it insanity?

SPARACIO: Insanity. Nobody wins. Everybody's in a no win situation. This guy [Stanfa] must be beside himself. . . .

AVENA: I mean, where is there any kind of . . . presence of brains? To go injure this young kid. No matter where you stand.

SPARACIO: Absolutely. Absolutely. Family, you know, was always taboo. There's no brains behind nothing. Maniacs. See, everyboy's got so many problems, like New York. . . . There's nowhere you can turn to make

sense out of anything. Before, people mediated things,
ironed something out. I don't know where the fuck it's
gonna lead. . . .

(Later)

SPARACIO: In all the years, in fifty years, there was always some kind of mediator, something. Something
could have been done. Something. This . . . I don't
know where the fuck it's gonna lead. It's a no win situation.

AVENA: Sam, it's not only here.

SPARACIO: Yeah, it's everywhere. That's what I'm saying. It's, it's not comfortable nowhere.

(Later)

AVENA: Guys like maybe your father, my father, they
would drop dead they see something like that.

SPARACIO: No question about it. Christ, they would have
rather died. They would have gave their life for their
principles. They would have gave their life in a minute
for their principles. . . . I tell you, I'm totally demor-
alized now. I thought for once . . .

AVENA: Sam, that's inexcusable. That's like me having a
beef with you, and I mean that kind of a beef, and I go
look to hurt your grandchild or your wife or somebody. I mean, where the hell these people come from?

SPARACIO: There's no . . .

AVENA: Then, then they deserve a grinding.

SPARACIO: Absolutely. Absolutely.

AVENA: Do you know what a grinding means?

SPARACIO: Yeah, you know, what it's gonna do is make
people desperate to go out and do something and it cre-
ates more . . . and now you gotta just really blow your
top and go out and, without patience, you know, and
you could send for something. . . . Completely demor-
alizing all the way around. Makes you wish you were
never near none of this. You know, for once in my life
I feel that I wish I, you know . . .

AVENA: Yeah, sure.

SPARACIO: In fact, my wife says, she wanted to move to

Florida. She can get a good job there. I don't know. I just . . . no light at the end of the tunnel.

After his son was shot, Stanfa was concerned with only one thing.

Revenge.

He wanted Merlino and anyone around him dead. Among other things, he ordered Gaeton Lucibello's teenaged son murdered in retribution.

"A son for a son," he said, in one of several meetings held in the stairwell of the hospital down the hall from where Joe Stanfa was recovering.

"There was to be no mercy shown," Sergio Battaglia later told the feds of those hospital meetings.

"John was in a rage. John wanted results. He didn't care if we got kids or wives. . . . He didn't want nobody to come back until they got results."

Not everyone thought this was the best strategy, but no one was about to mention that to Stanfa.

In one cryptic conversation picked up on September 7, Avena told Piccolo and Sparacio that Stanfa was refusing to provide police with a statement about the ambush. This, Avena implied, might not have been the smartest course of action. Clearly Stanfa and his son were victims and the more prudent position would have been to discuss the incident with investigators. That was what former mob boss Angelo Bruno, a man respected in both underworld and law enforcement circles, would have done, Avena said.

"I'm not the one to say," said Avena, who was called to the food warehouse when police first tried to question Stanfa on the day of the shooting. "He makes the decision. I think Ange would have handled it differently."

A little later the feds picked up what would prove to be the last conversation from Avena's office. The lawyer and Anthony Piccolo discussed the arrest of Phil Colletti in New Jersey four days earlier on a gun possession charge. That arrest, like so many others at the time, came after a traffic stop—this one by the New Jersey State Police.

The gun charge in itself was a minor affair. Everyone recognized that. But Avena said he was concerned because Colletti, whom he represented, had not called him. Both he and Piccolo were concerned that Colletti might have decided to cooperate.

"I'm not looking for something that has an odor," Avena said, "but Christ you better, you gotta have your nose in the air . . ."

"Scares you sometimes, Sal," Piccolo was heard responding, "when you think about it."

Concern about informants and concern about FBI bugs and surveillance were topics that cropped up frequently in conversations among those, like Piccolo and Avena, who met in the lawyer's office. The agents listening from the courthouse a block away got a big laugh one afternoon when they heard Avena explaining how he had spent $300 to have an electronics expert sweep his office for bugs.

"It's money well spent," Piccolo had said, as the tapes continued to roll and the conversations—despite the sweep—continued to be recorded.

"We were never worried," said Jim Maher, the FBI agent in charge of the investigation. "We knew they'd never find the bugs."

Whether that was a testament to the sophistication of the FBI equipment or the incompetence of the electronic sweeper, Maher wouldn't say. But for nearly two years, the FBI audio surveillance went on unimpeded.

That Stanfa and the others were suspicious was clear from their actions. There were whispered conversations, conversations in Italian, and conversations in hushed tones with a television blaring in the background. There was even one cramped meeting in the men's room of Avena's law office where Stanfa formally introduced Battaglia to Piccolo as a made member, or "amico nostro."

The bugs, first in the conference room, later in Avena's office and eventually in most of the rooms throughout the second floor suite, picked up most of what went on.

But on September 8, 1993, nearly two years after it was planted, the conference room listening device began to malfunction. Two days later, the bug in Avena's office also shut down. Under the terms of the court order, the bugs in the other rooms could not be activated unless the conference room and Avena office bugs were functioning.

Over the next few days, video surveillance continued at 519 Market Street and agents saw, at different times, Piccolo, Sparacio, and Joe Licata, the Newark-based mobster, arrive and depart Avena's law office.

"No monitoring was attempted because the microphones in Salvatore Avena's office and the conference room were not functioning," read a ten-day report later filed with US District Court.

The feds considered seeking court approval for another break-in in order to repair or replace the equipment. But with a grand jury already up and running, with Biagio Adornetto testifying, and with several other in-

formants feeding investigators information, the decision
was made to close down the audio and video surveillance at Avena's law office. The taping had gone on for
more than 500 days over a twenty-four-month period.
There were more than 2,000 conversations recorded. It
was, and remains, one of the biggest and longest-running
electronic surveillance operations ever conducted by the
FBI.

Now it became a deadly game of hide-and-seek. Hit
teams from both the Stanfa and Merlino organizations
were out looking for one another.

Veasey, who led the charge for the Stanfa side, was
part of a crew that used walkie-talkies and codes to communicate with one another as they set up ambushes for
Steve Mazzone and Mike Avicolli, identified by the feds
as two of Merlino's top associates. Other targets included Ron Galati—who owned a local auto body shop
where, Stanfa believed, the van used in the Schuylkill
Expressway shooting had been altered prior to the hit—
George Borgesi, Marty Angelina, and Gaeton Lucibello.

Veasey and his cohorts would refer to one another as
"Mickey Mouse" and "Donald Duck" on the walkie-
talkies. And when they wanted to know if a potential
target had been spotted, they would ask, "Have you seen
any Goofies?"

They also played mind games with one another.

Veasey got Merlino's beeper number and routinely
left messages for the rival gangster.

Once, when Merlino dialed the return number on his
beeper, the voice on the other end answered, "City
morgue." On several other occasions the return calls
went to local funeral homes.

"He was getting crank called all the time," said an associate. "They were trying to scare him."

At the time, the smart money was on Stanfa. The mob boss had more men and more firepower. And, given the way things played out over the next three months, it seemed like the safe bet.

The conventional wisdom was that the Merlino faction had blown its one chance to win the war when the hit on the Schuylkill failed. Had Stanfa been taken out, things might have been different.

But Stanfa wasn't dead.

He was pissed.

In the weeks that followed, three more mobsters were targeted and one, a Merlino associate named Frank Baldino, was killed.

Senseless doesn't begin to describe the hit.

Baldino, in his fifties, was a friend of Merlino's, but it was unclear even to law enforcement authorities whether he was involved in the young mobster's racketeering activities.

To Stanfa, it didn't matter.

A bartender and bon vivant, Frankie Baldino was the quintessential South Philadelphia streetcorner good guy, always ready to help a neighbor, always willing to go out of his way for a friend. During the day, he ran a clubhouse at Thirteenth and Porter Streets where some of the older guys from the neighborhood played cards and where, for a time, Merlino and his young associates hung out. Baldino would be found on most sunny afternoons sitting in a beach chair on the sidewalk outside the clubhouse soaking up the sun. He was tan from May to October.

At nights he tended bar, a job he loved because he

got to meet and talk with so many people. Bar owners loved to hire him because he had a following of regular customers who would stop for a drink wherever he worked. Bartending, his pretty young girlfriend, and a cappella 1950s doo-wop music were the passions in Baldino's life, said friends and family members after he was gone.

That he died in a mob war was totally out of character. But at the time, anyone linked in any way to Skinny Joey was on Stanfa's hit list. The standing orders were kill on sight.

Baldino had just finished dinner at the Melrose Diner, a popular restaurant in the heart of South Philadelphia, when he was spotted by Martines, Veasey, and Giuseppe Gallara, a young mob wannabe. It was a Friday night, September 17, 1993.

A light rain was falling as Baldino hustled out of the diner and slipped behind the wheel of his late model Cadillac. That's when Veasey and Gallara ran up on him.

"Yo Frank," Veasey hollered.

When Baldino looked up, Veasey pumped several shots into his chest and neck. Gallara, three steps behind Veasey, fired several more times into the hapless victim. Then the two triggermen ran around the other side of the diner and up a block where Martines waited in the getaway car.

That night an excited Veasey telephoned Phil Colletti.

"Yo bo," he said. "Home run. Turn on the radio."

The Baldino murder seemed to stagger both the neighborhood and the Merlino faction. Enough was enough. Police were pressured by community groups to crack down on the wiseguys. Traffic stops intensified. And

Merlino and most of his top associates went underground, avoiding their regular haunts and taking a decidedly low profile.

One, however, gambled for what he mistakenly thought would be a better future. Gaetano "Tommy Horsehead" Scafidi, whose brother Sal was doing forty years for racketeering, approached Stanfa and said he wanted to switch sides. Scafidi brought a list of all the bookmakers and loan sharks from whom the Merlino faction was collecting a street tax as a bargaining chip.

Stanfa, always on the lookout for the "river of money," welcomed the young mob turncoat with open arms. Veasey wasn't as willing.

"Two weeks ago we were trying to kill this guy, now we were supposed to kiss him," Veasey said disdainfully. "I wouldn't do it."

What Veasey and other members of the organization did do, however, was fill the vacuum created when Merlino and his crew pulled back. Now it was Stanfa's turn to pick up the spoils and, despite his claim that he wasn't going to twist arms, violence and threats became the calling cards of the organization. Sometimes it was subtle, as the FBI heard when James Pirollo, a local bookmaker from Northeast Philadelphia, agreed to wear a wire after he was approached by a Stanfa henchman named Jack Manfredi. And sometimes, when Veasey was involved, it was violently brutal.

**Pennsylvania State Police Surveillance Tape
September 20, 1993
8:45 P.M.**

JAMES PIROLLO: Hey, sit down. What's goin' on?
JACK MANFREDI: Nothin' . . . Stanfa sent me up here.

PIROLLO: Who sent you up here?

MANFREDI: Stanfa.

PIROLLO: Stanfa? For what.

MANFREDI: Ah, somebody gave him a list of names. He asked me if I know certain interests. I said yeah, I know this guy, JP. . . . What he's doin' now is he's, he's taking over. With everything that's going on right now in the city.

PIROLLO: That's nuts, what's going on.

MANFREDI: I know. Well, this is what's happening. Everybody took care of them other guys and they spit in their face and they never did nothin' for them guys. This guy's runnin' things the way it should be done, but he also wants everybody to pay him a little bit of respect. He's not trying to rape anybody. He wants money from every bookmaker in the city and he wants anybody that's doing any illegal business in the city to turn into him, or give him a piece. Because you see, see the difference between him and the other guys, when he says something he backs it up and he does something. These other guys are pieces of shit. They're shootin' anybody. But we don't have nothin' to do with them. . . . He just asked me to talk to you like a businessman and decide what you wanna do.

PIROLLO: It's ridiculous. It's even ridiculous to come up here for Christ's sake, you know.

MANFREDI: It's not my doing. I'm just telling you . . . the list was brought up. . . . Look, I'm not tryin' to come up here, look, I know you got family. I ain't tryin' to be no tough guy . . .

PIROLLO: I mind my own business. I'm a small guy, you know what I mean?

MANFREDI: Right. Well . . . then you give him something small if you decide that you wanna give him something.

Pirollo stalled and avoided Manfredi for several weeks after that first recorded encounter, but was confronted

again about two months later in a meeting outside a hotel
in Philadelphia.

**Pennsylvania State Police Surveillance Tape
November 23, 1993
8:15 P.M.**

MANFREDI: You're in business, you gotta do the right
    thing. Ain't no ifs, ands or buts, alright? That's it . . .
PIROLLO: What are you talking about?
MANFREDI: You gotta give us three hundred a week.
    Three hundred a week.
PIROLLO: Three hundred a week?
MANFREDI: Yeah.
PIROLLO: That, that's insane for Christ sake. Come on,
    Jack.
MANFREDI: Then get out of business.
PIROLLO: Right.
MANFREDI: Well then, get out of business. . . . You don't
    want no trouble right? We don't want no trouble.
PIROLLO: Well . . .
MANFREDI: This business, this business is our business,
    okay? Anything going on in this city is our business,
    okay? You're part of that business, you gotta do the
    right thing. Don't you understand the way it's been
    before you were born and before I was born. That's
    bullshit. It's gotta be done the right way. We want the
    money and that's, that's final. You don't want us
    comin' up here. You don't want no trouble. Do the
    right thing, okay? . . . Everybody's doin' the right
    thing. You can't be no different. I told you this the last
    time. . . . Ain't no talkin' no more. That's it. It's the
    last meeting. I'm tryin' to help you out.

Everybody had to do the right thing.

And the right thing was to give money to John Stanfa.

Veasey's method of collecting was a little different
than Manfredi's, however.

For several weeks, Veasey said, he had been trying to collect from a local bookmaker named Tony who had been pointed out as a major player in the video poker machine business by another Stanfa associate. Veasey said he, Battaglia, Keller, and "Johnny Gons" Casasanto had gone to Tony's house, knocked on his door, and demanded to see him. For a while he ducked and weaved, wouldn't come to the door, had his wife say he wasn't home. Finally, Veasey caught up with him outside a bar on Packer Avenue and delivered the message. Stanfa wanted $5,000 up front and a weekly payment of $300.

Veasey said he wanted the money by the end of the week. If not, he told Tony, "I'm gonna beat your ass."

The week ended without any payment.

A few days later, Veasey was out with his crew shaking down another bookmaker named Carmen on Thirteenth Street when Tony drove by. Veasey forced him to stop his car, a brand new Cadillac. And then he extracted payment.

"I punched him in the mouth a few times," Veasey said. "Pulled him out of the car. Took his keys. Threw his keys down the sewer. Got a knife from Johnny Gons, cut all his tires, cut all the seats, made Xs in all the seats and the roof of his car. It was a new Cadillac."

Then Veasey told Tony, "That's five thousand dollars worth of damage." And he walked away.

Carmen watched, his mouth agape. He had been balking at a demand for $800 up front and a weekly payment of $200.

"Naturally, after he seen what I did to this guy . . . he paid," Veasey said.

*   *   *

Veasey's reign of terror extended beyond the extortion racket. Being a wiseguy had clearly gone to his head. He talked tough and acted even tougher. Eventually Martines and Stanfa came to realize they had created a monster and tried to eliminate him.

But for most of the fall and early winter of 1993, John Veasey was the biggest and baddest mobster in South Philadelphia, and he wouldn't hesitate to tell anyone about it. He was formally initiated into the crime family by Stanfa at a making ceremony held in a room at the Penn Towers Hotel near the Hospital of the University of Pennsylvania.

While other mob informants still talked with a degree of reverence about their initiation, Veasey was cavalier in his explanation of that most sacred of all Mafia rites.

He described how his trigger finger was pricked with a pin and how Stanfa used a piece of toilet paper to dab the blood. Then the balled up toilet paper was placed in his cupped hands and set on fire. While it burned, he was told to repeat the Mafia oath of allegiance: *May I burn like this piece of paper if I betray this family.*

But Veasey had a comment to make first:

"I said, 'You know, I already burned my hand one time for this family, I've got to burn it again?' Because, you know, I really didn't want to burn my hand again. It was already burnt."

Veasey said after he was initiated, Filipelli, the former Mister America, went through the same ceremony. Then Stanfa offered Veasey a glass of wine. But the ruthless hit man and newly minted wiseguy declined.

He had to report to his parole officer later that afternoon.

"I had to go give urine at five o'clock," he said.

Veasey also had trouble with some of the intricate and time-tested Mafia protocols, particularly the prohibition about identifying yourself as a made member. Traditionally, unless a mobster was introduced by another known Mafia member as a friend of ours—"amico nostro"—other made members had no way of knowing who was and who was not formally initiated into the family.

Veasey got into trouble when he bad-mouthed Shotsie Sparacio during a couple of shakedown attempts. Several targets said they were already paying Shotsie.

"Who the fuck is Shotsie?" Veasey said, insisting on payment.

Later he had to apologize.

"I found out Shotsie had been a member for a long time," he said. "I was wrong. I didn't know who he was.

"But how the hell are you supposed to know who's who? They don't want to tell you. So, I started telling people that I met, 'I'm in the Mafia. If you are too, tell me.' That's the way I did it."

Veasey's disdain for the formalities of the organization was matched by his violent temper and his bravado.

After he got involved "with this Mafia thing," he renamed his two pet dogs, a Rottweiler and a pit bull, "Al Capone" and "Frank Nitti." On the witness stand, a defense lawyer later asked him if it were true that he once fed the pit bull a live chicken.

"Nah," said Veasey, pausing briefly before adding, "it was a rooster." Then, by way of explanation, he said, "It was better than fightin' the dog."

To commemorate his mob hits, Veasey had a tattoo of a smoking .45 caliber pistol drawn on his back along with two bullets, one for the Mike Ciancaglini murder and one for Baldino. Over the top of the gun were written the words SOMEBODY TALKED, a reference to the poster that hung in Avena's law office that Stanfa loved. Under the gun were the words THE ENFORCER.

A few weeks later, Veasey, Battaglia, Keller, and Casasanto went back to the tattoo parlor and had Chinese symbols drawn on their calves. The symbols, when translated, meant FAITHFUL AND LOYAL, pledges of allegiance to Stanfa that both Veasey and Battaglia would eventually break.

Veasey also had several other tattoos that predated his mob days. On the witness stand, he was asked about most of them, including a devil's head on one side of his chest.

"Everybody asks about that," he said. "But I got a God's head on the other side."

Then he paused, looked over at the jury and, with an engaging smile, added, "Everybody has a good side and a bad side."

12

Stanfa and Martines tolerated Veasey because he was an effective killer. But they also knew that the way he handled himself could cause the organization problems. The burning of the car and his hand after the Merlino-Ciancaglini hit was just one example of underworld incompetence that had brought quick and unwanted law enforcement attention.

Veasey's tattoos and neighborhood boasting were two others.

Then there was the assault on Joe Fudge.

Fudge, according to Veasey, had been going around town bad-mouthing him, threatening to kill him.

So Veasey drilled him.

Literally.

That Fudge was a cousin of Martines's and thus fairly well connected was of no consequence. He had crossed Veasey and Veasey wanted to make an example of him.

"He had been coming around my house, bothering my mother-in-law and father-in-law, looking for me," Veasey said while never completely explaining the origins of the bad blood. "I told Mister Stanfa—because he was Martines's cousin I wanted to ask him—I told him I was going to bust his face open when I seen him."

Not long after that, he got the chance.

Veasey was sitting at home when his brother Billy beeped him from a bar where he had a job hanging wallpaper. When Veasey called back, Billy said Joe Fudge was in the bar talking bad about him again, saying if he ever got ahold of him he was going to kill him.

Veasey arranged to have Johnny Gons, who was also at the bar, bring Fudge to his house.

Before Gons and Fudge arrived, Veasey told his wife to take a walk. Then he got out his electric power drill, attached it to a fifty-foot electrical cord, plugged it in, and set the drill on his kitchen table.

Gons, Veasey said, lured Joe Fudge to the house by pretending that he was going to help him. But once he got Fudge to the door, Veasey said, Gons grabbed him by the neck and pushed him inside.

"I sat him down and smacked his face with the drill," Veasey said. "Then I started drilling him. I asked him, 'Are you here to kill me?' I drilled him a few more times. I stuck the drill in his chest and his legs, on the side of his head. I ripped his hair out. You know, I would pull out chunks of hair from the rotation [of the drill bit]. I hit him with a bat in the knee."

Finally, the drill bit broke.

Veasey then took a gun from Gons, chambered a bullet, and handed it to the bruised and bleeding Joe Fudge.

"I said, 'Go ahead. Are you here to kill me? Let me see if you've got the heart to kill me.' And he's like, 'No, no. Please. Please.' So I threw him out of my house. I said, 'Get the fuck out of here, you faggot.' You know, 'Go tell who you've got to tell.' "

Veasey said Stanfa and Martines eventually reprimanded him for the assault.

"They thought I went a little overboard," he said.

*   *   *

Veasey was being paid $500 a week by the Stanfa crime family at the time. Both he and Colletti, because of the "work" they had done, thought they ought to be receiving more.

Given the amount of cash he was collecting from the extortion rackets, tens of thousands of dollars up front and weekly payments of several hundred, Veasey knew he was getting the short end of the big money. Stanfa and Martines, he thought, were rolling in dough. Other members of the organization were making a thousand a week or more. Yet here he was, putting his life on the line every day and still struggling to make ends meet.

"I made more money workin' than I did in the Mafia," Veasey said.

And for what?

The question would haunt Veasey as federal authorities, now intensifying their street-level investigation, began to draw their net closed.

While Martines and Stanfa outwardly disdained Veasey's heavy-handed tactics, they were not above employing them themselves when necessary, especially if money was involved.

"Martines liked to be the tough guy," said a former associate. "He thought he was John Gotti."

But Martines was smart enough not to go bragging about it.

Still, word got around.

One of the people on the list that Tommy Horsehead Scafidi brought with him when he switched sides was a butcher and bookmaker who had been paying a street tax to the Merlino faction.

In the fall of 1993, Scafidi, Martines, and Sergio Battaglia paid a visit to the meat market where he worked on Seventh Street. Scafidi opened negotiations.

"You paid Joey, now you gotta pay us," he said.

The butcher looked puzzled, played dumb.

So Martines nailed him with a left hook, knocking the young butcher to his knees.

"Frankie knocked him out," Battaglia recalled. "The guy was in a daze."

Now Battaglia and Scafidi dragged the butcher to the back of his shop where negotiations were going to continue. Both thought the guy was about to take a beating.

But Martines had a better idea.

"Forget about it," he said as he nodded toward a meat slicing machine. "Turn that on. We're gonna cut his hand off."

The butcher, snapping out of his stupor, begged and pleaded.

Then he paid.

The probe of the John Stanfa mob came full circle in the fall of 1993. What started out as a gambling investigation on the campus of La Salle University back in October 1990 ended with a series of tapes made by informants working for the New Jersey and Pennsylvania State Police on two separate mob-linked gambling and loan sharking operations. Both state police agencies turned their evidence over to the US Attorney's Office, where it was incorporated into the Stanfa RICO indictment.

The Jack Manfredi shakedown of James Pirollo was just one example.

In fact, it seemed like everyone doing business with

the Stanfa mob that fall was wired for sound. Some even turned up on video.

The operator of Delilah's Den, a fancy adult cabaret where topless showgirls danced on tables and rubbed up against customers' laps for big tips, was targeted by the Stanfa organization. But when Battaglia went to the club on Spring Garden Street to pick up a $2,500 extortion payment, the feds filmed him coming and going.

When Joe "Joey A" Altimari, a veteran mob bookmaker, put the word out that Stanfa wanted everyone to kick something back, his words ended up, like Manfredi's, on a series of Pennsylvania State Police wires.

And when Martines and Vincent "Al Pajamas" Pagano, at Tommy Scafidi's urging, started doing business with James "Jamo" Lynch over in South Jersey, the state police were already in place.

Lynch, an underworld operative who dabbled in all manner of contraband, including drugs and guns, was working with New Jersey authorities in order to help a friend who had gotten jammed up in a big drug case. His rap sheet read like the history of a guy who had always lived life on the fringes of the underworld, and included one of the more bizarre shakedowns disclosed during the subsequent Stanfa trial.

Once, Lynch was forced to admit under cross-examination, he extorted money from a woman in Florida by killing her poodle, cutting off its head and stuffing the head into her refrigerator freezer. The terrorized woman, faced with the lowlife version of the classic offer she couldn't refuse, came up with the cash.

But in 1993, Lynch was working with law enforcement. He introduced an undercover state police detective posing as an Atlantic City bookmaker to Scafidi, and then sat back as the detective, who was wired, paid $1,000 for the mob's protection and promised much more.

Scafidi, not the brightest light in the underworld, was easily sucked into the sting, bragging on one tape about the muscle he could offer the "bookmaker" and scoffing at the notion that the guy might be a cop.

"Listen, I don't know you, I don't know who you are," Scafidi said in his best tough guy tone. "You could be a cop for all I know . . . I'm just telling ya, you could be the fucking cops . . . which I don't give a fuck cause if I get pinched, I get pinched."

Tommy Horsehead's lack of mental acumen was legendary in the South Philadelphia underworld. Nothing he did after joining the Stanfa organization changed that perception. Two years later, while pleading guilty to a racketeering charge that included the extortion of the undercover detective, he was asked by his sentencing judge what year he had graduated from high school.

"Senior year, your honor," Tommy Horsehead replied.

Several members of the Stanfa organization, like Previte, the ex-cop, steered clear of any deal in which Scafidi had a role, wisely anticipating that the young mobster was a problem waiting to happen. Martines and Pagano, on the other hand, jumped at the chance to make a score, blinded, like Stanfa, by the dollar signs.

That's how the two high-ranking members of the organization ended up in a South Jersey diner talking at length with Jamo Lynch.

On several tapes later played in court, Martines and Pagano outlined the status of the Stanfa organization for

Lynch, describing how John Stanfa had bested Merlino and was now in charge of the city. Lynch, wearing a body-wire, got it all. Pagano, an old Scarfo family associate who had recently returned to Philadelphia from Florida, boasted about how he was a capo—"I'm big goose now"—openly mentioned La Cosa Nostra, and said "organized crime in Philadelphia got the word that Pajamas is back."

In another conversation, Pagano said, "Me and Frank . . . are second and third in command. . . . If he (Stanfa) goes to jail, me and him are in charge."

"Then," he told Lynch reassuringly as the state police tape continued to roll, "you don't have to worry about nobody, you know."

At another meeting in the same diner, Lynch got Scafidi to talk at length about Joey Merlino and Michael Ciancaglini, the mobsters and longtime friends Scafidi had betrayed when he switched sides. Scafidi told Lynch that Merlino and Ciancaglini had been greedy, that they collected extortion payments but refused to turn anything in to the organization. That's what caused the original rift with Stanfa, he said. Lynch, an underworld gossip of the highest order, had mentioned in another conversation that the word on the street was that Mike Ciancaglini and Joey Merlino had stashed three million dollars. The figure seems outlandish, but was indicative of the rampant and wildly speculative rumors swirling around the underworld at that time.

In fact, those who knew Merlino said he usually spent more than he ever earned and that he and Ciancaglini stiffed several bookmakers for tens of thousands of dollars by simply refusing to pay when they lost a bet. That, however, didn't put any money in their pockets—it simply made them deadbeats. But given their reputations, no one would say that to their faces and few bookmakers had the guts to turn down their action.

Whatever the facts, Lynch seemed to enjoy leading Scafidi on as he recounted, in almost soap opera fashion, the trials and tribulations of the Merlino faction and the star-crossed history of the Ciancaglini family. Michael Ciancaglini was killed, Scafidi told Lynch, because he and Merlino had been behind the hit on Joey Ciancaglini.

New Jersey State Police Surveillance Tape
December 15, 1993
10:27 A.M.

SCAFIDI: Take these kids Michael and Joey, man. They did the same thing. They did the same thing.

LYNCH: Yeah, well I heard they wasn't turning nothing in, man.

SCAFIDI: Nothing.

LYNCH: They were keeping it. Then they were going around saying they were the boss and the underboss.

SCAFIDI: Boss and underboss.

LYNCH: I, but, you know, I'm gonna tell you what, what was said to me on the street. I don't know how true it is. I don't. But I heard Michael had Joey done. You know what I mean?

SCAFIDI: Oh. Mike Chang. His brother.

LYNCH: Yeah.

SCAFIDI: Yeah, I heard they hated each other. I mean, ah, Michael hated, Michael hated him.

LYNCH: Yeah. I heard that. . . . Man, I said, what the fuck.

SCAFIDI: Heard the same thing. I know. But he, he hated his brother.

LYNCH: Yeah, but you know, he's still your flesh and blood here, man.

SCAFIDI: I know. Going to kill your brother. That's real
    nice.
LYNCH: That father must be pulling his hair the fuck out.
SCAFIDI: That's what I, that's what I was thinking. Even
    my brother said, I'd like to know what Chickie, you
    know . . .
LYNCH: Oh, he must be brokenhearted, man.
SCAFIDI: Then he went around, in the newspaper, the
    same exact thing I read in the newspaper. Mike, Joey
    [Merlino] was going around telling everybody Mike
    was the boss and he's the underboss.
LYNCH: I see that in the paper. That's what I heard
    about. But the thing, the other thing, I heard was, ah,
    from the street. Like from down, couple people I saw.
    I couldn't believe it at first. I said, ah.
SCAFIDI: It's a disgrace isn't it? Disgrace. That's why
    he's dead.

That Merlino hadn't joined the late Mike Ciancaglini
was still a major concern of Stanfa's. But by the time
Scafidi was gossiping with Lynch, Skinny Joey was well
out of everyone's reach.

On November 15 he was picked up by federal agents
and charged with violating his parole. It seems the video
camera mounted outside the clubhouse at Sixth and
Catharine Streets—the one that didn't pick up the August 5 ambush—did provide authorities with something
to pin on Skinny Joey.

Merlino had been placed on parole after serving two
years of a four-year sentence for the 1990 armored truck
robbery. He had been reporting to his federal parole officer on a regular basis and showing time cards indicat-
ing when and where he was at work soliciting business
for an aluminum siding company.

But FBI surveillance photographs and videos showed

Merlino associating with known felons, a clear parole violation. The videos also demonstrated that on several occasions when Merlino's worksheet indicated he was out soliciting customers, he was, in fact, in his clubhouse hanging out with the young wiseguys who surrounded him. Finally, the feds charged, an informant—Biagio Adornetto—had told a grand jury about Merlino's secret 1992 initiation into the Mafia, a ceremony that took place four months after he was released from prison.

This, the feds said, was another violation of parole.

On November 23, U.S. District Court Judge Norma Shapiro ordered Merlino back to jail. The sentence got him off the streets, out of the line of fire, and may have saved his life.

"Have a nice holiday, your honor," the ever charming Merlino told the judge as he was being led out of her courtroom in handcuffs.

Merlino spent that Thanksgiving and Christmas in a federal prison.

Stanfa, for perhaps the last time in his life, spent both holidays at home.

On December 7, 1993, John Stanfa celebrated his fifty-third birthday with a party at the Italian Cafe, a restaurant in Northeast Philadelphia that he frequented. The joint was well known to the FBI. Before it opened, it was the spot where Stanfa and Battaglia planned to lure Joey Merlino, Mike Ciancaglini, and Gaetano Lucibello for the "meeting" where they would be killed, the meeting where Stanfa planned to cut out Lucibello's tongue and where Battaglia planned to pour acid all over their bodies.

Filming from an unmarked van in the shopping center

parking lot where the restaurant was located, federal authorities recorded the arrivals and departures of more than a dozen members of the organization who came to pay their respects to Stanfa at the party. Every major player made an appearance for the feast which marked not only the boss's birthday, but also the family's success over the Merlino faction.

Battaglia, Keller, Veasey, Johnny Gons, and other members of their crew chipped in and bought Stanfa a $10,000 Rolex. They had it inscribed: "To John from Your Boys." Pagano and Martines showed up with a handsomely appointed, top-of-the-line twelve-gauge Remington shotgun. Nothing but the best for the boss.

With Merlino jailed, Stanfa was sitting unchallenged atop the underworld. He was anxious to cash in on the opportunities that lay before him. Bookmakers, loan sharks, drug dealers, and gamblers all over Philadelphia and South Jersey were being tapped and told it was time to pay their respects. The money was rolling in. Stanfa had cash hidden all over the Continental warehouse, Battaglia later told authorities—wads of bills, tens of thousands of dollars.

Three weeks later, John Veasey called the US Attorney's Office and began negotiating a plea agreement. Twelve days later he strapped on a body-wire and recorded a conversation with Stanfa and Filipelli. And two days after that, in an apartment atop a butcher shop in South Philadelphia, he took two shots to the head and one to the chest.

To everyone's surprise, he lived to tell about it.

The party was over.

* * *

John Veasey contacted the feds and said he wanted to cooperate on December 30, 1993. Encouraged by his older brother, Billy, and by several other family members, Veasey had a lawyer friend arrange a meeting with an Assistant US Attorney.

Barry Gross, the veteran prosecutor who was working the Stanfa case, got the call that afternoon. Minutes later Veasey and the lawyer arrived at the office of the Organized Crime Strike Force on Chestnut Street a block from the federal courthouse.

"You gotta picture this guy," Gross said. "He looks like John Belushi, right. He's wearing a watch cap. He needs a shave. But then he starts talking. . . ."

Gross knew the case against Stanfa was solid. He had coordinated the bugging and knew how powerful the taped conversations would be when played in open court. What's more, there already were several cooperating witnesses, including Adornetto, in the government fold. A grand jury had been reviewing evidence for months.

But Veasey was something special.

"Wait till you hear this guy," Gross told colleagues excitedly. "You won't believe it."

Veasey now says that he decided to cooperate because he felt guilt over the murders he had committed and because his brother Billy was pressuring him to straighten out his life. "I couldn't sleep. I was havin' nightmares," he said.

But from the underworld, there is a different story.

There Veasey is described as a remorseless "lowlife junkie" who was out to save his own skin. He had been stealing money, pocketing some of the shakedown payments he was collecting for Stanfa, and thought he was going to be killed because of it. Rod Colombo, he knew, had paid a similar price.

He also realized that he might be indicted for murder and could face the electric chair. So he decided to cut a deal and turn on his partners before someone else made the move and he was left out in the cold.

Some of that may have been true. It is a question that comes up whenever a murderer—and there have been many in a series of mob cases over the past ten years— decides to turn informant and testify in exchange for a lighter sentence. Leonetti and Gravano are the two prime examples, but in fact there have been dozens.

Prosecutors say it is a trade-off. Defense lawyers say it is an abuse of the judicial system. And on the streets, where legal issues are debated at a more realistic level, they say it is a way to get away with murder.

"The shooters are going to walk," family members said repeatedly during the Stanfa trial. "The ones who pulled the trigger are going to go free while my (husband, son, father, brother—the title changed depending on who was doing the talking but the message was always the same) goes to jail."

"What gives the government the right to grant a dispensation for murder?" asked an outspoken Merlino associate and close friend of the late Michael Ciancaglini. "What are they, the pope?"

On January 11, 1994, John Veasey got his dispensation, signing a cooperating agreement and a plea bargain. He also volunteered to wear a wire and record conversations for the FBI. On January 12, he was supposed to tape a meeting with Martines and Pagano, but they failed to show up. Later he met and recorded a conversation with Stanfa and his bodyguard, Vince Filipelli, the former Mister America.

It is unclear from that tape whether Stanfa and Filipelli suspected Veasey was cooperating with authorities. In retrospect, given what happened, you could read more into the comments. But at the time, no one picked up on it.

Stanfa knew there was an investigation going on and that the feds had some cooperating witnesses. He also knew that FBI agents were routinely stopping members of his organization and warning them that they might have a problem, that someone was out to kill them, implying that the contract might be coming from Stanfa himself. He also believed the feds were leaking information to the media, generating stories about an impending indictment to put added pressure on the organization.

It was all, Stanfa said, an attempt to sow discontent, to scare people into cooperating.

"See, I deal with a lot of lawyers," he told Veasey. "Everybody told me they gonna be indictment coming." So Stanfa said he wanted everyone to take a low profile "because the more noise, the more we stir, more stink coming up.

"They use every little hair they can use. Because my belief is they don't have it. They don't have too much . . . "

"So they're looking for shit," Veasey said.

"In other words, they have, you know, little things," Stanfa explained. "Here and there . . . Right now, see what they do, they make, in other words, they put on TV, they put it on the radio, newspaper. You know why? Because they trying to scare people."

"Make them run," said Filipelli.

"This way, they make and then, you know, they watch you, who, who they think they coming a little weak. Boom. They grab, and they say, 'Oh, they got a contract on you. They gonna do this. They gonna do that.' Because they want more people to talk. You know what I mean? That's why, you know, less people see I do something, less they know, better we are."

Later, Stanfa offered this assessment of the government probe:

"Believe me . . . you know, I just go by what I hear, from one lawyer to another lawyer. They . . . they no have a real full dish of spaghetti."

It was the last significant conversation the feds would tape of the mob boss and it was quintessential Stanfa. He had been underestimating the government probe and overestimating the intelligence of those around him for nearly four years. Now he was about to pay the price. He sealed his fate two days later when he ordered John Veasey killed. Like so much else that happened during Stanfa's brief and bungled tenure, the hit was botched.

On the afternoon of January 14, 1994, three days into his undercover assignment for the FBI, John Veasey taped a conversation with John Casasanto. Later that afternoon, he turned his taping equipment and a gun over to the FBI. He was supposed to meet again with the agents the next morning. In the meantime, he was told to lay low and try to avoid contact with anyone.

"I was supposed to be cautious, but not suspicious," he said.

Veasey had a small corner variety store near Seventh and Washington Streets, around the block from his house. He used the store as a hangout. He had a poker machine in there to generate some income and kept candy, cigarettes, and some other basic neighborhood necessities on the shelves. He was just closing the store that night when Martines and Pagano pulled up in a car and asked him to "take a ride" with them.

The night before, unbeknownst to Veasey at the time, FBI agents tailed him when he went out to a nightclub. They kidded him about it the next morning, asking pointedly about a red light he had driven through.

"I figured the FBI, they followed me the night before . . . so I figured maybe they was still following me or whatever," Veasey said.

They weren't.

Martines drove to the Warwick Hotel in Center City, where he said he had to meet someone. The three mobsters sat in the hotel bar for half an hour, sipping Dewars and water and watching a hockey game on the television. Then Martines got a message on his beeper, made a phone call, came back into the bar and announced they were leaving.

"Come on, I'll drop you off," he nonchalantly said to Veasey.

Veasey thought he was going home. Instead, he was driven to a butcher shop on Seventh Street. Martines had the key to an apartment on the second floor. He and Pagano said they wanted to show him how to manage a numbers operation that the mob was running out of that location. They said they wanted Veasey to work there for a while.

"We're gonna show you a numbers joint real fast," Pagano said. "This way you can keep a low profile if the cops are all over you."

Martines, after fumbling with the key, got the door unlocked and the three mobsters went upstairs. It was a small efficiency apartment. There was a couch covered with a tarp, a table and some chairs, a tiny kitchen area. Off to one side was a bathroom.

Pagano motioned for Veasey to sit down at the table. He then pulled out a yellow legal pad and started writing down some figures, explaining how the numbers business worked. Martines said he had to take a piss.

Veasey was sitting with his back to the bathroom door, looking at the numbers Pagano was writing on the pad. Then he heard Frank Martines say, "Bye-bye John."

Two shots rang out. The back of Veasey's head began to sting. He jumped up, turned around and saw Martines holding a .22 caliber pistol.

"Yo Frank, what the fuck are you doing?" he said.

Veasey was stunned. His eyes were blurry. He struggled to focus. Martines and Pagano, on the other hand, were shocked. At this point, if things had gone according to their plan, Veasey should have been slumped at the table and they should have been wrapping his body up in the tarp that covered the couch. But here he was standing in front of them, angry, confused, and still very much alive.

Pagano grabbed Veasey from behind and hollered for Martines to shoot him again. Martines fired, this time into Veasey's chest. Still, he did not go down. Instead, Veasey grabbed Martines and shoved him against the wall.

"I seen him slide the gun-stay back," Veasey said. "I figured the gun was empty. I backed up. Al pulled me. I had a three-quarter length leather jacket on with a hood. He pulled the jacket down over the top of my arms, so my arms was stuck . . . I couldn't do nothing.''

Martines started to pistol-whip Veasey, smashing the gun into the side of his head. Veasey managed to free his left arm. Every time Martines hit him with the gun, Veasey countered with a punch to Martines' face.

"You're dead, you're dead,'' Martines hollered.

"Not yet, I ain't,'' Veasey shouted back between blows.

Finally the gun slipped out of Martines's hand, bouncing off Veasey's head and onto the floor. With that, Veasey broke free of Pagano, grabbed Martines and shoved him down the stairwell. Martines broke his fall by grabbing a railing along the wall.

Veasey then turned on Pagano and the two crashed into a chair. Martines was back in the room throwing punches and hollering for a ''fair fight.'' He landed a shot squarely on Veasey's nose, breaking it. Blood splattered over the floor. Veasey jumped at Martines and flung him onto the floor, where he began to pummel him in the face with both fists. Pagano was back up and grabbing Veasey from behind by the hair.

In his hand he held a knife. He was trying to cut Veasey's throat.

Veasey sprung up and got his back to a wall. Now Pagano was coming at him with the knife from one side and Martines was moving in from the other. Pagano lunged first and Veasey reacted instinctively, kicking at the knife in the mobster's hand.

It fell to the floor. Both Veasey and Martines dove for the weapon. Veasey got there first and, in one motion, grabbed it and lashed out, ripping a gash into the side of Martines's cheek.

Everyone was breathing heavily, circling one another, moving into position. Veasey held the knife.

"Just calm down," Pagano said. "You know, we'll say we got jumped by some niggers. We'll go to the hospital."

"I'm not going anywhere with youse," Veasey said, fighting to catch his breath, struggling to stay alert and focused. His head and chest were throbbing. His nose was clogged with blood.

He told Pagano to go downstairs and unlock the street-level door to the apartment. Pagano again suggested they all go to the hospital, but Veasey wanted no part of it. Pagano said if Veasey put the knife down, he would open the door. Martines, bleeding badly now from his face wound, looked on.

First the door, then the knife, Veasey said.

Pagano went downstairs and opened the door. When he came back, Veasey plunged the knife into the back of the couch and bolted down the stairs, shoving Pagano as he ran by.

"You tell anyone about this and we'll kill your family," he heard Pagano scream as he careened down the stairs and out onto Seventh Street. Veasey sprinted a block, then collapsed on a stoop in front of a rowhouse.

"A black woman saved my life," Veasey said. "Her name was Tootsie." Tootsie called the cops.

"Help me. Get me to a hospital. I'm dying," Veasey moaned as he lay in a police van, its siren wailing, en route to Thomas Jefferson University Hospital. In the emergency room, where a team of doctors and nurses worked on him, Veasey was asked if he knew who shot him.

"Frank Martines," he said.

More police and FBI agents would interview him over the next two days, first in the intensive care unit and then in a heavily guarded hospital room. On that first night, when organized crime investigators got to him at the hospital, Veasey had tubes down his throat and up his nose. He was unable to speak. But he was awake, lucid, and able to tell his story by writing it all on a piece of paper attached to a clipboard held by a police detective.

By 6 A.M. the next morning, arrest warrants were issued for Martines and Pagano. The next day the two men turned themselves in to police. A lawyer who represented Martines at a preliminary hearing tried to dismiss the incident as a fight between friends.

"If this was a hit, this man Veasey doesn't get out of that room alive," said the lawyer.

It was a logical assumption. But those who had tracked the mob for the past four years knew that logic did not apply when it came to the Stanfa organization.

Mala fortuna. It hung over Stanfa like a dark cloud.

Two days after being rushed to the hospital and admitted in critical condition, John Veasey left with the FBI. His head hurt, he had a pain in his chest, and his vision was still a little blurry. But he was out of danger.

Two weeks later, he made his first appearance before a federal grand jury, the first hit man to turn. Shortly after that, Philip Colletti and his wife, Brenda, also cut deals with the feds and began spilling their guts to the same grand jury.

On March 17, 1994, John Stanfa and twenty-three of his top associates were indicted on racketeering charges that included murder, murder conspiracy, extortion, arson, kidnapping, gambling, and obstruction of justice. Among the mob plots was the attempt to kill John Veasey.

By that point, even Stanfa realized the government had a full dish of spaghetti.

"I guess I was the cheese," Veasey said.

13

The series of arrests on Saint Patrick's Day 1994 marked the end of the first phase of the Stanfa probe. For the next eighteen months the mob boss and most of his top associates would be housed in a federal prison in Fairton, New Jersey, as the case wound its way to trial.

Twice the indictment was expanded to add additional defendants. Ultimately, twenty-seven people were charged with conspiracy and racketeering under the Mafia-inspired Racketeering Influenced and Corrupt Organizations (RICO) Act.

And along the way, several defendants were removed from the case. Thomas Rebbie, a mob associate, agreed to cooperate and joined Adornetto, Veasey, and Phil and Brenda Colletti on the growing government witness list. Several others copped pleas, deciding it was better to concede guilt on lesser gambling and extortion charges and avoid the potential maximum sentences attached to a RICO conviction. One of the first was Tommy Morrone, the bulky young mob collector whose confrontation with Eddie O'Hanlon on the La Salle campus set the investigation in motion. Others pleading guilty before trial included Gary Tavella, Gaetano Scafidi, Ron

Mazzone, Vince Filipelli, Jack Manfredi, Joe Altimari,
and Johnny Gons Casasanto.

Meanwhile, on the streets, the Philadelphia mob was
undergoing yet another reorganization. Ralph Natale, the
man Stanfa wanted killed, the man he didn't even want
to give time to breathe, was released from federal prison
in September after serving nearly seventeen years on
federal arson and narcotics charges. Joey Merlino came
home a month later after doing a year for parole violation.

By the end of 1994, federal authorities were drawing
up a new organization chart for the Philadelphia branch
of La Cosa Nostra. Natale, they said, was the boss. Merlino, who had opened a coffee and cigar shop on Passyunk Avenue, was the underboss. And both, said the
feds, were being supported by the powerful Genovese
crime family out of New York. In fact, some investigators believed, the Philadelphia family was now little
more than a satellite, a branch office for the biggest and
most circumspect mob family in America.

The sixty-six-year-old Natale, it was said, got his
marching orders directly from Vincent Gigante. And
Merlino was in line one step behind him. The vacuum
created with the indictment and arrest of Stanfa and most
of his top associates was quickly filled. And much to
the chagrin of the imprisoned mob boss, those doing the
filling were the two men he had desperately wanted to
kill.

But that was only one of the major embarrassments
for Stanfa as he sat behind bars awaiting trial. In May
1995, as federal authorities were planning a trip to Italy
to depose Fernando Vincenti, the waiter kidnapped by
Tavella and Rosario Bellocchi, Bellocchi cut a deal. The

move shocked everyone involved with the case, including Bellocchi's court-appointed lawyer, who had no idea his client was about to flip.

For Stanfa it was the ultimate betrayal.

Bellocchi, after all, was one of his own, Sicilian-born and personally recruited by the mob boss. On top of that, Bellocchi was engaged to marry Stanfa's daughter. He had been brought into the family and The Family. His defection was a public humiliation, as shocking as a slap in the face to Stanfa. All his talk of honor, loyalty, and the ways of La Cosa Nostra appeared to be little more than hollow posturing as his organization crumbled around him.

"I guess this means the engagement's off," quipped one wiseguy still on the streets when word of Bellocchi's defection began to circulate.

With Tavella pleading guilty and Bellocchi cooperating, the trip to Italy to depose Vincenti seemed unnecessary. Still, Deputy US Attorney Joel Friedman pushed ahead.

So it was that for five sunny days late in May, Friedman, Assistant US Attorney Paul Mansfield, FBI Agent Paul Hayes Jr., ten defense attorneys, defendant Luigi Tripodi (one of the few permitted bail in the case) and two newspaper reporters from Philadelphia encamped in Lecce, a small city in the province of Puglia, deep in the heel of the Italian boot.

There, in an Italian courtroom closed to the press, Vincenti was deposed. Once again the waiter offered a conflicting and not particulary enlightening account of his abduction. When it was over, he stood outside the public courthouse in the warm Italian sunshine and shook hands with the defense attorneys as they headed back to their hotel.

"It's okay, right?" asked the waiter, who clearly wanted nothing more to do with the Philadelphia mob.

In fact, the deposition recorded in Italy was never played at the Stanfa trial. It wasn't needed. The trip, at government expense, seemed superfluous. But for Friedman and those in his office who had been tracking and prosecuting mob cases for nearly two decades, the effort was as important as the result. It really didn't matter what Vincenti said or that his testimony proved irrelevant. The point that Friedman made was simply this: his office would go wherever it had to go and pay whatever price it had to pay to build its case against La Cosa Nostra.

An anonymously selected jury began hearing testimony in the Stanfa case late in September 1995. First the government played a series of tapes, then came the witnesses. Then more tapes. Then more witnesses. It went on for nine weeks.

Jim Maher, the FBI agent who headed the investigation, was one of the first. Paul Hayes was also called to the stand to explain, among other things, the chilling audio- and videotape of the hit on Joe Ciancaglini.

While the Ciancaglini shooting was not one of the charges listed in the indictment, it was part of the mob war that was the backdrop of the case, and prosecutors wanted the jury to see and hear what that war was really like.

The tape lasted no more than fifteen seconds, but it seemed to capture the jury's attention more than any of the lengthy conversations in which Stanfa and the others were heard discussing mob business. It also dramatically underlined the point that the prosecutors, Friedman, Gross, Mansfield, and Robert Courtney, stressed throughout the nine-week trial. Despite the talk of honor and loyalty, despite the Hollywood and media-hyped image of glamor and glory, the Mafia is about cold, ruthless acts of violence and a wanton grab for power and money.

If that wasn't clear, the point was made again out on the streets of South Philadelphia as the trial moved into its second week. On the morning of October 5, the day John Veasey was scheduled to take the witness stand, his older brother, Billy Veasey, was shot and killed a few blocks from his home. The murder, a message from the mob, caused a three-day recess in the trial.

Billy Veasey was on his way to work that rainy morning when two men ran to his four-wheel drive vehicle as it turned onto Oregon Avenue near Seventeenth Street. The gunmen pumped a half dozen shots into the chest and body of the thirty-five-year-old Veasey, who died in a hospital less than an hour later.

No one has been charged in the murder, which is still under investigation by both Philadelphia homicide detectives and the FBI. The initial theory was that the shooting was an attempt to intimidate John Veasey. And that, indeed, may have been part of it.

But there was apparently more than one reason for the hit. Billy Veasey, according to several sources in both law enforcement and underworld circles, continued to operate on the fringes of the South Philadelphia underworld even while his brother was a cooperating witness. He had recently had a run-in with a major South Phil-

adelphia bookmaker tied to the mob and was also said
to be running his own gambling and loan sharking operation.

"He thought he was a big shot," said one underworld
figure. "He used to brag about his FBI connections. Because of his brother, he thought he could do whatever
he wanted."

There were, investigators believe, as many reasons for
the murder as there were bullets fired that morning.
Whether it was an attempt to help Stanfa, however, is
open to speculation. Those running the mob—Natale
and Merlino—had no reason to do anything that might
undermine the prosecution of the deposed mob boss. But
those running the mob would certainly benefit, investigators believed, from anything that discouraged cooperation in the future.

The murder of Billy Veasey, then, might have been a
message designed to reestablish order in the underworld.
This, the shooting said, is how informants and the families of informants will be dealt with in the future.

It was a crude and violent version of *omertà*.

Revenge, the Sicilians say, is a dish best served cold.

John Veasey, whose paternal heritage was hazy but
whose maternal bloodlines ran to Palermo, had been
waiting nearly two years to even the score with Stanfa
and Martines when he finally took the stand on October
11, 1995.

They had tried to kill him.

They might have had a role in the murder of his
brother.

Now, he was going to settle accounts.

"He's more determined than ever," a friend of

Veasey's said when asked if the death of his brother had caused him to rethink his decision to testify.

For nearly three days, first on direct and then under cross-examination, Veasey recounted the story of the mob war and his role in it. Later, four of the jurors in the case said his testimony—coupled with the tapes— were what made the case.

"It was like he was standing on a corner telling a story," one juror said. "He was sincere, down to earth, you know. He was believable."

He was the hit man who wouldn't die, the tough-as-nails South Philadelphia streetcorner hustler who took two bullets to the back of the head and one in the chest and lived to tell about it.

For two and a half days he sat on the witness stand and talked—not like a witness, but like a guy sitting on the stool next to you in the corner taproom. Talked not like a killer, which he was, but like the black sheep in your family; the irascible cousin who always gets in trouble or the thrice-divorced uncle who can't hold a job but who sits center stage whenever the family gets together for dinner. Roguish charm is the phrase that comes to mind.

There have been more mob witnesses in Philadelphia than in any other city in America. They have set the standard for informant testimony. But John Veasey took it to another level.

Colorful, dramatic, profane, Veasey charmed the jury. There's no other way to describe it. He offered no excuses. Put on no airs. He was what he was, plain and simple. And now he was willing to tell all about it.

"A couple of the lawyers tried to catch him up in

semantics," Paul Hayes said after an initial round of cross-examination. "John doesn't even know what semantics means."

But he knew all about the murders and the murder plots and he regaled the jury with the story, sprinkling in his own asides, telling stories about his tattoos and his pet dogs and his rocky marriage.

With a large round face and thick, dark hair, he did, in fact, look like the late John Belushi, the actor-comedian. In fact, Veasey brought a lot of Belushi to the witness stand; the same cockeyed glance and quizzical smile, the charming bad-boy twinkle in the eyes, the disarming, can-you-believe-it shrug. He was the Samurai Hit Man, the Blues Brother who became a wiseguy.

And his tales of botched and bungled murder attempts, of bombs that failed to explode, of stolen getaway cars that wouldn't start, of the hit he called off because he had an appointment with his parole officer, and of his own irreverent making ceremony sounded like a script from Saturday Night Live.

Then, in the middle of it all, during the talk about murder and mayhem and blood and beatings, there was a reference to his mother, who had been dead for several years. And John Veasey, the hit man, paused on the witness stand, made the sign of the Cross and said quietly, "God rest her soul."

The trial was over after Veasey finished testifying. Even some of the defense attorneys privately conceded that. But it would drag on for nearly two more months. More tapes. More witnesses. More staggering testimony. Phil Colletti corroborated Veasey on several key issues. Brenda Colletti was devastating as a backup witness to both her husband and Veasey. Bellocchi, with his thick Sicilian accent and bewildered naivete, was even better.

It was an overwhelming case in which the defense could offer little by way of rebuttal.

Frank Martines tried, however.

In a bizarre outburst that seemed to underscore the futility of the defense, he rose to refute the testimony of Colletti, who had been going on and on about the treachery and deceit that was at the heart of the Stanfa organization.

"Your best friend is usually the one they get to kill you," Colletti said, noting that Martines had lured Veasey to a meeting and then shot him.

With that, Martines jumped up from his seat at the defense table and shouted out, "John Veasey was *never* my best friend."

Then Martines quietly sat back down as the judge, the jury and the lawyers looked on in amazement.

The verdict came in a little before noon on November 21, 1995.

Sitting at the defense table next to his lawyer, John Stanfa never flinched.

Stone-faced, he turned briefly to his wife, son, and older daughter sitting two rows behind him in the packed courtroom, put a finger to his lips, then mouthed the words, "Don't cry."

The women, Lena and Sara, were sobbing quietly.

Joe Stanfa, like his father, stared straight ahead.

It took the jury forewoman nearly fifteen minutes to read all the charges and announce all the findings. Stanfa and Martines faced life in prison without parole. The other defendants were looking at between thirty and eighty years.

With friends and family members looking on, some stunned, others crying uncontrollably, Stanfa and his co-defendants, the hierarchy of an organization he had taken three years to build and less than six months to run into the ground, were led off in handcuffs.

Outside, in the glare of television cameras and amid a swarm of reporters, Friedman, Gross, Mansfield, and Courtney praised the jury and the justice system, the FBI, the other law enforcement agencies, and the witnesses for the devastating victory over La Cosa Nostra.

"It is a proud day for law enforcement," Friedman said.

But it was Louis Pichini, head of the criminal division of the United States Attorney's Office in Philadelphia and a former Strike Force Attorney himself who gave perspective to what the prosecutors and FBI had accomplished not just at the trial, but during the entire grueling four years of preparation and investigation that led to it.

They had, Pichini said, shown the American Mafia for what it is today.

"You pierce the veil and what you find is a bunch of street thugs with no sophistication," Pichini said. "They're really no different than these neighborhood drug gangs. . . . We give them names and put them on charts, but they're really no different."

After years of successful investigations and prosecutions like the one that brought Stanfa down, the American Mafia, Pichini said, "is a shell of what it once was."

Epilogue

Less than two months after the convictions, Sergio Battaglia cut a deal with the government and began co-operating. By the end of January 1996 he was being debriefed in anticipation of taking the witness stand against five other Stanfa case co-defendants who were about to go on trial.

Much of what he had to say about the mob war and the plots to kill Joey Merlino and his associates was a rehash of the testimony of Veasey, Colletti, and Bellocchi. But the young wiseguy added significant details about the murders of Rod Colombo and Mario Ricco-bene and talked for the first time about Stanfa's desire to kill two defense attorneys and a newspaper reporter. He also offered secondhand information from conversations with Gaetano "Tommy Horsehead" Scafidi about the Merlino faction's involvement in the ambush of Joey Ciancaglini and in several other unsolved gangland shootings, including the murder of Felix Bocchino.

Battaglia's first appearance in court came during the

trial of Salvatore Avena, Luigi "Gino" Tripodi, Salvatore Brunetti, Giuseppe Gallara, and Gaeton Lucibello
that began in March 1996. The case was tried in the
same seventeenth-floor courtroom where Stanfa and his
co-defendants were convicted. And for the most part, the
government presented the same evidence, playing many
of the same tapes and calling many of the same witnesses. Battaglia's was one of the few new faces on the
witness stand.

This time, however, there was a significant defense.

Three of the defendants, Avena, Tripodi, and Lucibello, took the witness stand. All three adamantly denied
the charges. What's more, Avena's lawyer, Edwin Jacobs Jr., did a masterful job of using the government's
own tapes to support his argument that Avena was acting
as a lawyer, not a mobster, when he met with Stanfa and
the others.

Jacobs was able to show that Avena wasn't in the
room when most of the criminal conspiracy discussions
took place and that his client was clearly a victim of a
mob power play in the controversial trash dispute that
was central to most of the discussions on which he was
recorded.

Tripodi testified that he was a onetime friend of
Stanfa's, but never a member of his mob. His lawyer
went even further, arguing at one point that Tripodi had
a brief fascination with the mob that brought him into
Stanfa's orbit. It was, the lawyer said, a sort of midlife
crisis for the then-fifty-five-year-old Tripodi. Some men
get a divorce and chase after young women, the lawyer
told the jury. His client chased after the Mafia.

Lucibello insisted that he was not a member of any
criminal organization. And both he and his attorney

played off the fact that even the government's tapes portrayed him as a target, not a co-conspirator. Lucibello, after all, was the man whose tongue Stanfa wanted to cut out, put in an envelope, and mail to his wife.

The trial lasted nearly three months and ended with a split decision. Lucibello was found not guilty of all charges. Avena was acquitted of the most serious racketeering charge, but the jury hung on two other counts. Gallara and Brunetti were found guilty. And the jury hung on all three counts—racketeering, racketeering conspiracy, and obstruction of justice—against Tripodi.

Several months later, the prosecution decided to drop the two remaining charges against Avena. While the official reason was a somewhat convoluted legal explanation, most people felt the fact that jurors had deadlocked eleven-to-one in favor of acquittal was reason enough not to retry that part of the case. The prospect of having to face the tenacious Jacobs in court again also may have been part of the equation.

A second Tripodi trial ended with yet another hung jury. Federal authorities then decided to drop the more serious racketeering charges against the restaurateur. In August 1997, at a non-jury trial that lasted one day, he was tried and acquitted of an obstruction of justice charge. Another defendant in the Stanfa case, Santo Bravata, was arrested in Italy in the summer of 1996 after having been a fugitive for nearly two years. He was extradited to the United States and eventually pleaded guilty to a racketeering conspiracy charge.

In all, twenty-four of the twenty-seven defendants indicted in the Stanfa investigation were either convicted or pleaded guilty. Three—Avena, Lucibello, and Tripodi—were acquitted.

On Tuesday, July 9, 1996, John Stanfa was sentenced to five consecutive life terms by Judge Ronald Buckwalter following a brief hearing in the same courtroom where the trial was held. Stanfa's wife, several friends and family members, and a few reporters were on hand for the twenty-minute proceeding.

While it capped one of the most devastating investigations of organized crime in the history of the city, it was in many ways anticlimactic. Stanfa wore an orange prison sweatsuit. He was deeply tanned and appeared unconcerned. "No thank you," he said when asked by Buckwalter if he had anything to say before sentencing. While being led back to jail in handcuffs, he turned and smiled at his wife and gave a thumbs up sign to a friend.

His lawyer said he would appeal the conviction.

At separate sentencing hearings Frank Martines was sentenced to life, Vincent "Al Pajamas" Pagano got eighty years, Anthony "Tony Buck" Piccolo and Raymond Esposito each got got forty-five years, and Salvatore "Shotsie" Sparacio got thirty years. The numbers really didn't matter. Given their ages and their health problems, Pagano, Piccolo, Esposito, and Sparacio were, like Stanfa and Martines, sentenced to spend the rest of their lives behind bars.

As a result of his cooperation, Battaglia was sentenced to ten years. At this writing he remains in the protective custody wing of a federal prison, where he is visited on a regular basis by FBI agents and state and federal prosecutors who are trying to build additional cases against what is left of the organization. Veasey was also sentenced to ten years. Colletti was sentenced to twelve and a half years. And Bellocchi was given fifteen years.

*   *   *

In November 1996, Joey Merlino came off probation. For the first time in nearly a year, the travel and association restrictions that he had been living under were lifted. Now he could go wherever he pleased with whomever he pleased. Within days he hosted a lavish party at the posh Ben Franklin House in Center City Philadelphia. More than three hundred guests turned out for the affair, a belated celebration of the baptism that summer of his four-month-old daughter.

Merlino and his girlfriend Deborah were host and hostess for the reception-like party that began at 5 P.M. and lasted well into the next morning. Two orchestras, a string band and a disc jockey provided nonstop entertainment. The banquet opened with hot hors d'oeuvres and champagne. Then they brought out the entrees— pasta, calimari, scampi, king crab legs, filet mignon, veal chops, and porchetta. After midnight they served a buffet breakfast.

It was the underworld social event of the year. Cops, federal agents, and a half dozen television camera crews and newspaper photographers were on hand to record the arrival of the guests. It looked like the Academy Awards.

Later Merlino would complain about the attention, about the invasion of his privacy. ''I don't bother nobody, I don't want nobody to bother me,'' he said in a rare newspaper interview. ''Did I do something wrong?''

Federal and local investigators tried to paint the party as a coming out for the young mob boss and hinted that members of several New York crime families were in attendance. Members of the Gambino, Lucchese, and

Bonnano crime families were there, investigators said, to pay their respects.

One local mobster, however, said the cops and the media had it all wrong.

"Sometimes a party is just a party," he said.

Two weeks later, Joey was at it again.

For the second year in a row, on the Tuesday before Thanksgiving, he staged a dinner and Christmas party for the homeless. The first party was on November 21, 1995—the day Stanfa was convicted. While the party had been planned weeks in advance and Merlino had no way of knowing when the jury would return its verdict, the timing was perfect for the young wiseguy.

"He's smart, but he's also lucky," said a former Stanfa cohort of his onetime nemesis. "And in this business sometimes lucky is better."

STANFA CONVICTED and MERLINO FEEDS HOMELESS were matching headlines in newspapers and on television reports. It was a classic South Philadelphia moment. A year later, Merlino put on an even bigger spread for about sixty adults and children from a homeless shelter. They were bussed to a Passyunk Avenue restaurant up the street from Merlino's coffee shop. A string band greeted them at the door, serenading their arrival. Upstairs in the banquet room a buffet Thanksgiving dinner was set out. There were a dozen neatly set tables for the guests. In one corner of the room was a Christmas tree, and underneath it were stacks of gaily wrapped boxes, gifts for each homeless person in attendance.

But there was more.

Along the wall, lined up and arranged by size and color, were twenty-two brand new bicycles—from twelve-inchers with training wheels for the youngest of the homeless to twenty-six-inch black dirt bikes for the teenagers.

Merlino, wearing a brown suit over a stylish black shirt, was the polite and benevolent host. After dinner Santa Claus arrived and distributed the gifts. The kids went crazy. The string band played Christmas carols. A half dozen of Merlino's associates sang along. Joey Merlino smiled.

"These people are hungry and we gave them something to eat," he told one television reporter. "If you were hungry, I'd do the same for you."

Federal authorities saw both the big bash at the Ben Franklin and the lavish spread for the homeless as examples of Merlino's brash, in-your-face underworld style. "He thinks he's Al Capone or John Gotti," said Jim Maher. "But look where they ended up. Capone died of syphilis and Gotti's gonna die in jail."

Merlino, in response, said if the feds had a case, they should bring it on. "I'm not going anywhere," he said.

A month later, just before Christmas, Joe Sodano turned up dead in Newark. Sodano, a capo who controlled the Philadelphia mob's North Jersey gambling and loan sharking operations, was found slumped behind the wheel of his four-wheel-drive vehicle in the parking lot of a nursing home on Newark's north side. He had been shot twice, once in each side of his head. He was fifty-eight.

Police believed he had been lured to a meeting by an associate who set him up for the kill. Sodano, who had served two years in prison on a state racketeering charge, had been out of jail about a year. A major moneymaker for the organization, he had been aligned with Stanfa at the start of the 1993 power struggle with the Merlino faction, but had missed most of the action because of his state prison sentence.

When Sodano came out of jail things had changed dramatically. Stanfa was out of the picture, and those he had wanted dead were now in power. What's more, members of the powerful Genovese organization were said to be casting an envious eye toward the lucrative video poker machine distribution network Sodano controlled in North Jersey and New York City.

Sodano might have been able to buy himself some time, but that was apparently against his nature. "He always made a lot of money," a former associate said of Sodano. "But he didn't always spread it around the way he should."

Some investigators looked at the Sodano shooting as the last act in the Merlino-Stanfa war. Others saw it as a bloody first step in an underworld reorganization. Sodano left behind a pile of money and a lucrative and well-organized gambling and loan sharking operation. But his real legacy, in law enforcement circles at least, was the jaded and cynical view of La Cosa Nostra that the FBI captured in the first significant conversation recorded in Sal Avena's law office on December 3, 1991.

"Ego is a dangerous thing," Sodano had said during that classic sitdown in which he, Stanfa, and Piccolo talked about the problems that were plaguing the American Mafia and complained about the arrogance and incompetence of the younger generation of gangster.

"There are so many things that . . . I don't know how to straighten them out," Sodano said.

Then he added what, five years later, could have been his epitaph.

"I don't care what other people do," he said. "I'm not going to change my principles. I don't give a fuck. . . . Whatever happens, happens."

JOHN STANFA: We don't want quantity, we want quality. . . . Joey, believe me, what I know, what I see. Lot of people, they no even belong near us.

JOE SODANO: You're right.

STANFA: Because who, who done one thing, they done another thing. Because that guy maybe they can bring, you know, a thousand dollars, two thousand dollars. I don't got no money, Joey. I no hungry for money, either. Because This Thing, This Thing it's not for money. . . .

Rogue's Gallery

SALVATORE AVENA—lawyer whose Camden, New Jersey, offices were bugged by the FBI for two years beginning in October 1991. Charged with racketeering along with mob boss John Stanfa and twenty others in 1994. Tried and acquitted of racketeering in 1996. Jury hung on two other charges, conspiracy and obstruction of justice. Charges were later dismissed.

BIAGIO ADORNETTO—pizza maker and wannabe wiseguy whose unwanted romantic pursuit of mob boss John Stanfa's daughter nearly got him killed. Became the first member of the Stanfa organization to cooperate with federal authorities.

FRANK BALDINO—South Philadelphia bon vivant and longtime friend of Joseph "Skinny Joey" Merlino. Gunned down outside the Melrose Diner in September 1993 in a hit carried out to avenge the shooting of John Stanfa's son, Joe.

SERGIO BATTAGLIA—young mob figure convicted of racketeering-murder charges with Stanfa and six others in 1995. Later cut a deal and began cooperating with federal authorities. Admitted his role in more than a dozen murder plots.

ROSARIO CONTI BELLOCCHI—Sicilian-born hitman who was engaged to marry Stanfa's daughter, Sara. Pleaded guilty to racketeering-murder charge after becoming a cooperating government witness. Testified against Stanfa and other top mob figures.

SANTO BRAVATA—Sicilian-born bricklayer and friend of mob boss John Stanfa. Fled the Philadelphia area after being indicted for racketeering in 1994. Accused of taking part in two murder conspiracies. Arrested in Italy in July 1996. Extradited and pleaded guilty to a racketeering charge in 1997.

SALVATORE BRUNETTI—South Jersey mob associate and cousin of mob underboss Frank Martines convicted of racketeering-murder charges in 1996. Charged with helping to make the bomb used in plots to kill mob rival Joseph "Skinny Joey" Merlino and other Merlino associates.

JOHN CASASANTO—South Philadelphia mob associate who pleaded guilty to racketeering conspiracy charge, admitting his role in a murder plot and a series of extortions. Sentenced to ninety-seven months in jail.

JOSEPH CIANCAGLINI Jr.—reputed underboss of the Stanfa mob. Gunned down when three hitmen burst into his luncheonette early one morning in March 1993. Survived the attack, which was recorded by an FBI surveillance camera and electronic listening device.

MICHAEL CIANCAGLINI—brother of Joe Ciancaglini but member of rival mob faction headed by Joseph "Skinny Joey" Merlino. Shot and killed on a South Philadelphia street corner in August 1993.

BRENDA COLLETTI—wife of admitted hit man Philip Colletti. Pleaded guilty to an obstruction of justice charge after agreeing to cooperate with authorities. Testified against Stanfa and seven others in the 1995 racketeering trial that led to Stanfa's conviction.

PHILIP COLLETTI—admitted hit man, pleaded guilty to a racketeering-murder charge after agreeing to cooperate. Testified against Stanfa and Stanfa's co-defendants in 1995 racketeering case.

WILLIAM D'ELIA—identified by FBI and Pennsylvania law enforcement authorities as leader of the Bufalino crime family in Scranton-Wilkes Barre area. Picked up on tape in Avena's office discussing mob connections to the trash hauling business.

RAYMOND ESPOSITO—South Jersey mob figure and top Stanfa associate, convicted of racketeering along with the mob boss in 1995. Sentenced to forty-five years in prison.

VINCENT FILIPELLI—former professional bodybuilder who served as Stanfa's bodyguard. Pleaded guilty to a racketeering conspiracy charge, admitting his role in a series of mob extortions. Sentenced to fifty-five months in prison.

CARMINE FRANCO—trash company operator identified by FBI and US Justice Department as top associate of the Genovese crime family. His dispute with Avena over a trash company they co-owned was the topic of hours of mob talk picked up by FBI bugs in Avena's office.

GIUSEPPE GALLARA—South Philadelphia mobster convicted of racketeering-murder charge in 1996. Charged with being one of the gunmen in the 1993 Frank Baldino hit.

HERBERT KELLER—mob associate, close friend, and high school classmate of Sergio Battaglia. Convicted of racketeering charges with Battaglia, Stanfa, and five others in 1995.

GAETON LUCIBELLO—Merlino associate targeted for brutal death by Stanfa, who wanted to cut out his tongue and send it to his wife. Tried and acquitted of racketeering charges in 1996. Convicted of a gun possession charge .

JACK MANFREDI—mob-connected bookmaker. Pleaded guilty to racketeering conspiracy, admitting his involvement in extortion attempts. Sentenced to forty-one months in prison.

FRANK MARTINES—acting underboss of the Stanfa crime family. Convicted of racketeering in 1995 along with Stanfa and six others. Accused of attempting to murder John Veasey. Sentenced to life in prison.

JOSEPH MERLINO—reputed South Philadelphia mob leader who headed rival faction in 1993 underworld war with Stanfa organization. Shot and wounded in the August 1993 hit that left top associate Mike Ciancaglini dead. Currently described by federal and local law enforcement agencies as the underboss of the Philadelphia mob.

THOMAS MORRONE—low-level mob enforcer whose attempt to collect a gambling debt on the campus of La Salle University in 1990 set the Stanfa investigation in motion. Pleaded guilty to a racketeering conspiracy charge. Sentenced to twelve months in jail.

RALPH NATALE—Stanfa rival who emerged from prison in 1994 after serving seventeen years on drug trafficking and arson charges. Federal and local authorities say he now heads the Philadelphia mob with Merlino as his underboss.

VINCENT PAGANO—conspired with Martines in the Veasey hit. Convicted of racketeering along with Stanfa, Martines, and the others in 1995. Sentenced to eighty years in prison.

ANTHONY PICCOLO—veteran "gentleman" mobster. Served as Stanfa's crime family consiglière. Convicted of racketeering in 1995 case. Sentenced to forty-five years.

RONALD PREVITE—ex-Philadelphia cop who reputedly became a major player in the Stanfa organization, controlling gambling and loan sharking in the Atlantic County area.

SALVATORE PROFACI—identified by FBI as a capo or captain in the Colombo crime family out of New York. Son of the late Colombo boss Joe Profaci. Picked up in several bugged conversations discussing mob connections to a trash dispute between Avena and Franco.

GAETANO SCAFIDI—former Merlino associate who switched allegiance to Stanfa. Pleaded guilty to racketeering conspiracy. Sentenced to eighty-two months in prison.

SALVATORE SPARACIO—longtime South Jersey bookmaker. The original target in the investigation that brought down the Stanfa mob. Convicted of racketeering in 1995. Sentenced to thirty years in prison.

JOHN STANFA—Sicilian-born Philadelphia mob boss whose brief and bloody reign ended with his conviction on racketeering charges in November 1995. Sentenced to five consecutive life sentences.

GARY TAVELLA—South Philadelphia mob associate charged with a botched 1993 kidnapping attempt that was right out of *The Gang that Couldn't Shoot Straight*. Pleaded guilty to racketeering conspiracy charge. Sentenced to 90 months in prison.

LUIGI TRIPODI—Philadelphia-area restaurateur accused of being a capo or captain in the Stanfa mob. Tried twice on racketeering charges. Each trial ended with a hung jury.

JOHN VEASEY—admitted hitman. Pleaded guilty to a racketeering-murder charge. Was one of the shooters in both the Mike Ciancaglini and the Frank Baldino hits. Testified against Stanfa and the others in 1995 and at two other mob trials growing out of the investigation. Shot and wounded in 1994 while working with the FBI.

Compelling True Crime Thrillers